THE BIBLE OF THE REFORMATION

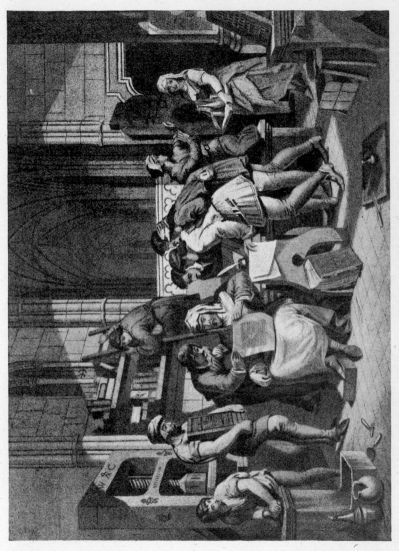

CAXTON READING THE FIRST PROOF SHEET

THE BIBLE OF THE REFORMATION

ITS TRANSLATORS AND THEIR WORK

BY THE

REV. W. J. HEATON, B.D.

FELLOW OF THE ROYAL HISTORICAL SOCIETY
AUTHOR OF "OUR OWN ENGLISH BIBLE"

WITH ILLUSTRATIONS AND FACSIMILES

SECOND EDITION

London:

FRANCIS GRIFFITHS

1913

THIS SECOND EDITION

IS

DEDICATED TO

MR. AND MRS. J. K. WADDILOVE

OAKHURST, MANNINGHAM

BRADFORD

CONTENTS

CONTENTS

LIST OF ILLUSTRATIONS

LIST OF ILLUSTRATIONS

THE BIBLE OF THE REFORMATION

BEING THE SECOND VOLUME
OF "OUR OWN ENGLISH BIBLE"

"The Schoolmen, having subtle and strong capacities, abundance of leisure, and but small variety of reading, their minds being shut up in a few authors as their bodies were in the cells of their monasteries ; they, with infinite agitation of wit, spun out of a small quantity of matter, those laborious webs of learning which are extant in their books. For the human mind, if it acts upon matter, and contemplates the nature of things and the works of God, operates according to the stuff, and is limited thereby ; but if it works upon itself as the spider does, then it has no end, but produces cobwebs of learning, admirable indeed for the fineness of the thread, but of no substance or profit."

BACON, *Advancement of Learning.*

"The Reformation is not to be regarded as a great and sudden event which took the nation by surprise. It was merely the crisis, to which things had been tending for some centuries. And if the fire did at last run over the country with wonderful rapidity, it was because the trees were all dry."—J. J. BLUNT.

THE BIBLE OF THE REFORMATION

CHAPTER I

WAS IT NEEDED ?—ERASMUS

IN our first volume, on the Manuscript English Bible, we have broken up fresh ground. No other work has ever dealt separately with this early period, so full of fascination. But the printed Bible has been discussed again and again; and, in venturing once more on such familiar ground, we are reminded of Pliny's remark, that it is no easy task to give novelty to what is old. But " the world moves," and so much has come to light quite recently. The *State Papers* are full of interest on such a subject. And the publication of the *National Dictionary of Biography* has thrown a flood of light on many of those whose labours will now be recorded. In particular, a somewhat full account of all who took part in the Bishops' Bible will be given. And are not the translators of the Authorised Version worthy of everlasting remembrance ? Their work has been published millions of times ; and it has influenced our literature, and our national life, for good, as perhaps nothing else ever did. Yet how few know anything about the men to whom we are so vastly indebted ? For, even in works on the subject, they receive only scant notice.

Pursuing, then, the history of our "rightful though interrupted inheritance," we now approach the Reformation period. Archdeacon Hare has said that Luther's intense love of truth, which could not be lulled by any

I

make-believe, is the legacy he has bequeathed to the Protestant Churches. But it was not he alone that was yearning after realities. The feeling was widespread, and only needed a powerful and consistent spokesman.

To glance briefly at the period preceding that of Luther and Tyndale, the most remarkable event was, of course, the invention of printing. About half-way down the fifteenth century, the secret, which now seems so simple, was discovered for Europe by a German. For, whilst

MEMORIAL TO THE FIRST PRINTERS, FRANKFORT.

many of the great inventions which have altered the face of society belong to our own country, this one, by far the most influential, was discovered in the country where the Reformation itself originated, and just in time for it.

About 1450 John Gutenberg began to print at Maintz, the first attempts having been at Strasburg a little earlier. He expended nearly all his substance on the invention, and was about to abandon it in despair, when, through the advice and assistance of John Faust, he was enabled to proceed. Peter Schoeffer, at first a servant, and afterwards a son-in-law, of Faust, discovered the readier method of casting the types; and they kept their secret for some time, till, at last, it was divulged by their workmen. The first book that appeared with a printer's name and date was the best-loved portion of the Word of God —the Psalms—as was fitting. It was printed at Maintz, in 1457. Beautiful from the first, the initial B was imitated in Dibdin's *Bibliotheca Spenceriana.* But, in twenty years, the colour faded; though the original, four hundred years old, is well preserved.

Just at the right time for the new art, the sack of Constantinople, in 1453, sent large quantities of the most valuable manuscripts broadcast over Europe; and thus both " knowledge and vital piety " were stimulated.

They met in Erasmus, whose Bible work parallels that of Luther. His *Praise of Folly* is a powerful satire on the absurdities of the period. Listen to his description of one of the sermons of the time. " I heard a grave divine taking upon him to treat of the mysterious name of Jesus, who did very subtilely pretend that in the very letters was contained whatever could be said of it. For, first, its being declined with three cases did expressly point out the Trinity of persons. Then, that the nominative case ended with s, the accusative with m, and the ablative with u, did imply some unspeakable mystery; namely, that, in words of those initial letters, Christ was the summus, or beginning; the medius, or middle; and the ultimus, or end, of all things." Erasmus says that the monks were wonderfully fond of the Fire of Purgatory, because it was so useful to their kitchens; but that, in many countries, the people scarcely heard a profitable sermon once in six months. " I am firmly resolved," he exclaims, " to die in the study of the Scriptures. In them I find my joy and peace." And again, with regard to the new learning of the time, he says: " The highest object of the revival of philosophical studies will be to learn to become acquainted with the simple and pure Christianity of the Bible."

Froude says that, when Erasmus's New Testament and

Paraphrase came out, the laity were able to see, side by side, the Christianity which converted the world, and the Christianity of the Church, with a Borgia Pope, Cardinal Princes, Ecclesiastical Courts, and a mythology of lies. Between 1526 and 1536, 30,000 copies of this New Testament were put into circulation ; and the *Manual of a Christian Soldier*, which Tyndale translated at Little Sodbury, was also a work of pronounced anti-papal tendencies. It said that Christianity was not a matter of the acceptance of dogma or the performance of outward ceremonies and rites, so much as a pure, righteous, and self-sacrificing life.

Simple and pure Christianity was, indeed, almost unknown in all Europe. Divines of eighty years of age were ignorant of quotations from St. Paul ; and preachers of long standing had never seen the New Testament. We are told that the Archbishop of Maintz said of the Bible : " In truth, I do not know what this book is, but I perceive that everything in it is against us." Cardinal Hosius's persuasion was that it had been best for the Church if no Gospel had been written. The maxims that were current at the time are decisive enough on the point.*

Even a little later, when Hooper was Bishop of Gloucester, out of 311 of his clergy, he found 168 unable to say the Ten Commandments ; 31 of these did not know where they were ; 40 could not tell where the Lord's Prayer was given, and 31 did not know the author.

Erasmus found the spurious gospel of Nicodemus chained to a pillar in the nave of Canterbury Cathedral, but no Bible. Meantime, there were far more Moham- medans than Christians, and the number was rapidly increasing.

The age was run mad on ceremony. Tyndale says, in his answer to More : " That trust which the ceremonies preached to be given unto God's word and Christ's blood, that same they turned unto the ceremony itself; as though a man were so mad, to forget that the bush at the

---

* " Quanto eris melior grammaticus, tanto pejor theologus. Græce posse scriptum fuerit. Hebraice proprie hereticum."

ERASMUS.

FROM THE ORIGINAL PICTURE BY G. PENN, IN HIS MAJESTY'S
COLLECTION AT WINDSOR.

tavern door did signify wine to be sold therein, but would
believe that the bush itself would quench his thirst."
And the expense of all these ceremonies was enormous.
Tyndale's language on such a subject is righteously strong.
"How cometh it that a poor layman, having a wife and
twenty children, and not able to provide for them, though
all his neighbours know his necessity, shall not get, with
begging for Christ's sake, in a long summer's day, enough
to provide for them two days honestly: when, if a disguised monster come, he shall, with an hour's lying in
the pulpit, get enough to provide for thirty or forty sturdy
lubbers a month long, of which the weakest shall be as
strong in the belly, when he cometh unto the manger, as
the mightiest porter in the Weigh-House, or the best
courser that is in the king's stable?"

The partial reforms that had taken place needed to be
carried much farther; and the pictures which stand out
most vividly in the fifteenth century have only one
interpretation. Innocent VIII. chasing and murdering the
Waldensian believers; John Huss, and Jerome of Prague,
martyred as if by barbarians; the monasteries filled with
the timid, the lazy, and the disappointed, though never
without a seasoning of the salt of the earth; the pulpit
largely given up to what was fanatical, or ridiculous, or
political; and, in many parts, scarcely employed at all;
while the whole system of Popery was used, mainly, either
for money-making or the gaining of secular power. Even
when men were dead, still money was demanded, that
masses might be said for their souls, which never went
either to heaven or hell, but always to Purgatory. In his
Obedience of a Christian Man, Tyndale says: "If a poor
man die, and leave his wife and half a dozen young
children, with but one cow to feed them, that will they
have for a mortuary, mercilessly; let come of wife and
children what will. Yea! let anything be done against
their pleasure, and they will interdict the whole realm,
sparing no person."

The Schoolmen, both Dominicans and Franciscans, also
contributed very largely, by their support of the existing

order of things, to its downfall.   We have described their ancestors, in the days of Wycliff.   Roger Bacon says: "The miserable herd of students fatigue themselves, and play the fool, about the miserable translations of Aristotle; and lose their time, their labour, and their expense. Appearances alone engage them, and they have no care to acquire real knowledge; but only to seem knowing in the eyes of the senseless multitude."

Hear Mr. Brewer on these Schoolmen:—

"They had pierced and drilled, by their vermiculate questions, the solid body of the general belief; until, under the guise of its defenders, they had become its most dangerous enemies.   Every form of difficulty or error, which had ever entered the brains of others or themselves, had been so carefully stated, and so laboriously confuted, that doubts, which might have died of themselves, or obtained, at best, a narrow and precarious existence, gained a fatal activity by their writings.   For, error is too subtle to yield to dialectics.   And, such is the perverseness of the human mind, that the poison remains, when the antidote is forgotten." *

Adrian vi., indeed (Pope, 1522–23), ingenuously confessed that great distress had justly come upon the Holy See, as a punishment of the abominations that had been committed in it; and he promised to carry out a reformation himself, despising Luther and all his party.   He died, however, before he had sat two years in the Papal chair; not without good suspicions of foul play.†   The Council of Trent was, in fact, the acknowledgment of crying grievances and corruptions; though its slow assembling, and long protraction, did not evidence any great desire to deal with them.   It was said, indeed, that there could be no reason to imagine that the grace of the Holy Spirit was present with such a council, except that the managers were brought to it with as much difficulty as if they had been sure to meet the Holy Ghost there.

---

* *State Papers*, vol. iii., Rev. J. S. Brewer, M.A.

† Somers' *Collection of Tracts*, vol. ix., "State of the Church of Rome when the Reformation began."

We must close this general sketch by quoting the words of Mr. Froude, who says: "Protestantism was a falling back upon the rules of truth and piety which lay upon the surface of the Bible: and a determination rather to die than to mock with unreality any longer the Almighty Maker of the world. Intellect, as it ever does, followed in the wake of the higher virtues of manly honesty and truthfulness."

CHAPTER II

WHAT ABOUT ENGLAND?

"Our grand business in life is not to see what lies dimly at a distance, but to do what lies clearly at hand."—CARLYLE.

BUT we turn to our own country, without attempting a more detailed description of the need of a sweeping reformation. That need was seen clearly enough within our own shores; but, perhaps, the full time had not come before the instruments were ready. Lord Macaulay, at least, is responsible for the saying that, corrupt as the Church of Rome had become, if it had been overthrown in the twelfth, or even in the fourteenth century, the vacant space would have been occupied by some system more corrupt still. Wycliff's work had never, indeed, died out; and Tunstall, Bishop of London, wrote to Erasmus, in 1523: "It is no question of some pernicious novelty. It is that new arms are being added to the great band of Wycliffite heretics." Erasmus, in the same year, said that the Wycliffite party was "not extinguished, but only overcome." They were still reading Bible fragments in barns and behind hedges, and keeping alive what has come to be the dominant force in Protestantism.*

Now, however, that the time had come, it seemed as if the Papal hierarchy was to illustrate its greatest pomp and pride immediately before its fall. Never had England had a representative of the Vatican who approached Cardinal Wolsey, both in outward grandeur and in real

---

* J. H. Gardiner, *The Bible as English Literature*. Chaucer, in his *Ploughman's Tale*, shows himself a thorough Wycliffite.

power.   In 1513 he was made Bishop of Tournay, in France; in 1514, Archbishop of York; in 1515, the King's High Almoner, Cardinal, and Lord High Chancellor of the kingdom; and, in 1518, the Pope's Legate.   His revenues, from all sources, were immense; and his style of living equalled that of the mightiest sovereigns.   On special expeditions he was attended by four thousand horsemen, including nobles, prelates, and knights; and

WOLSEY IN CHANCERY LANE.

the bosses of his mule's bridles might buy Christ and His Apostles, as the satire said.*

When at home, Wolsey's ordinary establishment, at Hampton Court, numbered a thousand persons.   At the head of his yeomen and ushers, there were nine or ten lords to wait on him, each with several servants; the Earl of Derby having five.   Attending his table, there were twelve doctors and chaplains, a physician, four councillors learned in the law, two secretaries, a herald-at-arms, a sergeant-at-arms, an armourer, and a Clerk

* "Rede me and be nott wrothe."—W. ROYE.

of the Green Cloth, etc. As Shakespeare says, he bound all England, by suggestion; and, though he probably never said "Ego et meus rex," he often said "My king and I." He was far more powerful than the Pope himself, says the Venetian Giustinian; though he was foiled in his attempts to reach the Vatican, through political complications. Who could have thought that he and his Church were so quickly to fall together! Amongst his last words were—"Commend me to His Royal Majesty, and request him, in God's name, that he be on the watch to depress this new sect of Lutherans; from whose mischief, God in His mercy defend us!" Six years later, Tyndale died, praying—"Lord, open the King of England's eyes."

Who, then, was Tyndale, whose prayer we know to have been answered? We may well call him one of the torch-bearers going first in this ever-memorable period. He it was who first gave the printed Bible to English people. Foxe calls him "the true servant and martyr of God, the Apostle of England in this our latter age." It is an indication of the state of religion, that no one should have attempted the work before. For the Mazarin Bible, a Latin copy, had been printed and sold seventy years before Tyndale commenced his labour.

The printing establishments of Gutenberg and Schoeffer were broken up by the sack of Maintz, in 1462; and their workmen, becoming dispersed, carried the new invention into almost every country of Europe. Moreover, translators were not wanting; so that, before the end of the fifteenth century, Bibles were printed in Spanish (1478), in Italian (1471), in French (1487), in Dutch (1475), in German (1467), and in Bohemian (1488); being all taken from the Vulgate. The Mazarin Bible was Gutenberg's work; and it was a splendid trophy of the new art. Hallam says : " It is a very striking circumstance, that the high-minded inventors of this great art tried, at the very outset, so bold a flight as the printing of an entire Bible; and executed it with astonishing success. It was Minerva, leaping on the earth in her

WOLSEY AT LEICESTE RABBEY.

13

divine strength and radiant armour, ready, at the moment
of her nativity, to subdue and destroy her enemies. We
see, in imagination, this splendid volume leading up the
crowded myriads of its followers, and imploring a blessing
on the new art, by dedicating its first-fruits to the service
of heaven." * The first portion of the New Testament
printed was the Hymn of Zacharias, and that of Mary;
which were printed as an Appendix to a Greek Psalter,
in 1486.

Apart from the ecclesiastical influences which hindered
the printing of the Bible in England, it is to be borne in
mind that never, within our shores, has the Sovereign
undertaken any expense in connection with it. In
Germany, two generations before the time of Tyndale,
a translation was commenced at the Imperial expense.
The Danish translation has been four times revised by
order of as many kings; and one King of Denmark
appointed a travelling commission for the collection of
manuscripts, at his own expense. The Swedish, Norse,
and other versions have also had public assistance. But
the English versions have been the result of independent
enterprise, though occasionally sanctioned by the reigning
monarch.

Connecting, then, the name of Coverdale with that of
Tyndale, by later references, let us glance at his personal
history, as it amply lies before us. William Tyndale was
born about 1484; being connected, in all probability,
with a baronial family. Demaus, in his second edition
(Lovett's edition), thinks that all the evidence is in favour
of Tyndale's being born at Melksham Court, Stinchcombe,
this being the home of Tyndale's family. It was another
family, of the same name, that resided at North Nibley;
though the memorial column has been erected there.†
Family legends are generally worthy of consideration,
and, according to them, the Tyndales came from the

* *Literary History*, edition 1864, p. 156.
† *W. Tyndale*, G. Barnett Smith. Full particulars of Tyndale's family
will be found in a little publication by B. W. Greenfield, Barrister-at-
Law, entitled *Notes relating to the Family of Tyndale*, London, 1878.

north, during the Wars of the Roses; and, to elude
observation, changed their names to Hutchins, or
Hychyns. Thus Tyndale entered Oxford as William
Hychyns. But, afterwards, the family reverted to their
former and rightful name of Tyndale.

WILLIAM TYNDALE.

Tyndale was educated, like Wycliff, at Oxford, "where
he increased, as well in the knowledge of tongues and
other arts, as especially in the knowledge of Scriptures,
whereunto his mind was singularly addicted." In his

days, great changes were constantly taking place in the thoughts and feelings of those who were influenced by the revival of letters. And in Oxford, naturally, such changes would find their surest register. Tyndale says, in his *Practice of Prelates*, that when he first went to Oxford most of the teaching pertained as much to the healing of a man's heel as to the saving of his soul; and that no one looked at the Scriptures until he had been trained in heathen learning for years.

Several Oxford students had been to Italy, however, and had learned to love and understand the Greek tongue, and to read the Bible instead of the Schoolmen. One especially, John Colet, had imbibed the spirit of the great Florentine reformer, Savonarola; and returned to begin at Oxford a movement which was to have an altogether immeasurable influence. Colet began to lecture on St. Paul's Epistles, studying them as any other letters might be studied, and quoting Plato, when he did quote, more than either Aquinas or Scotus. Sir Thomas More and Erasmus were powerfully influenced by him, being at Oxford at the same time. Thus, before many years were gone, the books of the Schoolmen, which had been so highly prized, became little more than waste paper.

Colet was the son of a Lord Mayor of London, and in course of time was appointed to the Deanery of St. Paul's Cathedral. More, Grocyn, Linacre, and other Oxford students were also found in London, when Erasmus visited it, in 1505. These men formed a powerful little group, who could not go on in the old ways; though they came, afterwards, to differ widely from one another. Colet was made Court Preacher on the accession of Henry VIII., and excited plenty of malice amongst the old school by his bold reforming spirit. Tyndale says, in his answer to Sir T. More's *Dialogue*, that Fitz-James, Bishop of London, would have made Colet a heretic, for translating the Pater Noster into English,* and denouncing the worship of

* Arber's Reprint.

images, but the Archbishop of Canterbury dismissed the charge as frivolous.

Colet preached, in fact, before the Convocation, and seized the opportunity of urging, in the plainest manner, the need for an improvement in the morals of the clergy. The wicked worldly life of some of the bishops, he averred, was far worse heresy than that of poor Lollards; two of whom had just been burnt at Smithfield.

Colet used his father's fortune to found the public school by the side of St. Paul's, in which "gentleness and prayer" were made much of, in place of the barbarous usages of the period; and in which the pure Latin and Greek imported from Italy were taught, as well as the "new learning" generally.* It became a model school, copied in fifty towns.

There was a widespread indifference, as a rule, however, at this period, and for some time afterwards, to any special dogmatic truths. And, except a man chose to obtrude his "heresies" in the very face of his bishop, he was safe enough. Mr. Brewer, the able editor of the *State Papers*, says: "In general, the indifference or contempt with which the bishops regarded departures from established doctrines, especially when the dissent was not attended with scholarship, was more galling, in many cases, than when they launched against it their ecclesiastical fulminations."

* *The Oxford Reformers*, Seebohm.

CHAPTER III

TYNDALE AT THE UNIVERSITIES, AND IN GLOUCESTERSHIRE

"He that has light within his own clear breast
May sit i' the centre, and enjoy bright day."

MILTON.

TYNDALE probably entered Oxford about 1504, and
became a student at Magdalen Hall, where Wolsey had
distinguished himself when little more than a boy. His
portrait hangs in the Refectory, with an inscription,
freely recognising his services as a translator, and his
virtues as a man and a martyr, and calling him the Pride
of the Hall and the Apostle of England.* In these early
days, he read privately to certain students and fellows of
Magdalen College, "some parcel of Divinity, instructing
them in the knowledge and truth of the Scriptures."
We are not surprised to learn, therefore, that he was
soon suspected of Lutheranism; and, after a time, he
found it desirable to move on to Cambridge.† There the
same influences would be found as at Oxford, and his
views would be confirmed by intercourse with some of
the leading spirits among the Reformers.

Though Erasmus had left Cambridge, it may have been
some teaching of his which first suggested to Tyndale the
noble design of giving his countrymen the Word of God.
We must dwell, at some length, on Erasmus's own New
Testament; so will only quote here his words in the

* Now Hertford College.
† "It is a mistake to suppose that Tyndale left Oxford for Cambridge
to sit at the feet of Erasmus; for he took his M.A. at Oxford in 1515,
and Erasmus had left Cambridge in 1514. See the preface to Lovett's
edition of Demaus's *Tyndale*.

19

Paraclesis: "I totally dissent from those who are unwilling that the sacred Scriptures, translated into the vulgar tongue, should be read by private individuals; as if Christ had taught such subtle doctrines that they can with difficulty be understood by a very few theologians; or as if the strength of the Christian religion lay in men's ignorance of it. The mysteries of kings it were perhaps better to conceal, but Christ wishes His mysteries to be published as widely as possible. I would wish even all women to read the Gospel and the Epistles of St. Paul. And I wish they were translated into all languages, of all people, that they might be read and known, not merely by the Scotch and the Irish, but even by the Turks and the Saracens. I wish that the husbandman may sing parts of them at his plough; that the weaver may warble them at his shuttle, that the traveller may, with their narratives, beguile the weariness of the way."

Luther's influence was great all over Europe, but he never came here, and the recent *Cambridge History of Literature* says very properly: "The English Reformation began at Cambridge, and the Cambridge movement began with Erasmus, although he was not its sole author." *
It was a great disappointment for him at first, his coming to England in 1509. His pupil, Lord Mountjoy, wrote telling him of the accession of Henry VIII., and assured him that being a humanist Prince, he would encourage learned men, without whom the rest of mankind would hardly exist. All things would be full of honey and nectar for him. Erasmus was poor, and came, to find that Henry took no notice of him. However, plenty of others did, and he became a notable teacher and writer, finding friends who delighted and surprised him here. He said of Colet that when he heard him, he seemed to be listening to Plato, and he assured the prior of the convent to which he was still nominally attached that there were as accurate scholars in Latin and Greek here as there were

* *Renascence and Reformation*, vol. iii., A. W. Ward, Litt.D., and A. R. Waller, M.A.

LITTLE SODBURY MANOR HOUSE IN 1839.

LESS DISTANT VIEW.

in Italy. His works had an immense sale and influence. Amongst the MSS. preserved at Corpus Christi, Oxford, there is the day-book of an Oxford bookseller, showing what he sold in 1520. His name was John Dorne, and he had sold 2383 books during that year, one-ninth of the whole being written or edited by Erasmus. Seventy-five editions of the *Enchiridion* were published in Henry's reign alone.

Bilney and Cranmer were both at Cambridge in Tyndale's time. Latimer was there also, though he was then a determined opponent both of Greek and the study of the Scriptures. Tyndale's somewhat long residence, in first one University and then the other, laid the foundation of that good scholarship which he afterwards evidenced in his translation; Sir Thomas More, his great antagonist, allowing that, before he left England, he was "well known for a man of right good living, studious, and well learned in Scripture." There never was, in fact, a word to say either against his character or scholarship.

From Cambridge, Tyndale proceeded to act as tutor in the family of Sir John Walsh, a Gloucestershire knight, whose manor house, amongst the Cotswolds, was picturesquely situated.* Here he could still devote a large portion of his time to study, his pupils being very young. In fact, he must have been more of a chaplain than a tutor, and would have plenty of time for thought.

It was while he was living at Little Sodbury that Tyndale's strong repugnance to much that was ecclesiastical, without being religious, manifested itself. In the dining hall (which can be seen to-day) there were accustomed to assemble many neighbouring priests; and, in their company, he began to express himself with great

* Being on the western side of the Cotswolds, the Forest of Dean is near at hand. It furnished oak for the navy; and the Spanish Armada was instructed to destroy it (*Tyndale*, C. Tylor, 1898).

The manor house at Little Sodbury is still to be seen, being now a substantial farmhouse, as I found one lovely summer afternoon, after taking the train to Yate.

LADY WALSH AND TYNDALE.

23

freedom Foxe says, that "as he was learned, and well practised in God's matters, so he spared not to show unto them, simply and plainly, his judgment. And when they at any time did vary from his opinions, he would show them in the book, and lay before them the manifest places of Scripture, to confute their errors and to confirm his sayings." At length his patrons undertook to expostulate with him on the subject, and the argument used by Lady Walsh shows that money power is no

CHAPEL AT LITTLE SODBURY.

modern metewand. "Why!" she said, "here is such a doctor as may dispend a hundred pounds; and another, two hundred; and another, three hundred pounds; and were it reason, think you, that we should believe you before them?" So that Hudibras was not far wrong :

"What makes all doctrines plain and clear?
About two hundred pounds a year.
And, that which was proved true before,
Proved false again? Two hundred more,"

Or Shakespeare:

> " O what a world of vile ill-favoured faults
> Look handsome in three hundred pounds a year ! "

It was here, however, that Tyndale avowed the resolu-
tion that, before many years, he would cause the boy
that drove the plough to know more of the Scriptures
than the priests themselves. "A thousand books," he
exclaims, "had they rather to be put forth against their
abominable doings and doctrines, than that the Scripture
should come to light. For, as long as they may keep
that down, they will so darken the right way with the
mists of their sophistry, and so tangle them that either
rebuke or despise their abominations with arguments of
philosophy, and with worldly similitudes, and apparent
reasons of natural wisdom, and with wresting the
Scripture to their own purpose (clean contrary unto
the process, order, and meaning of the text); and so
delude them with descanting upon it with allegories;
and amaze them, expounding it in many senses before
the unlearned lay people, when it hath but one simple
natural sense, whose light the owls cannot abide; that
though thou feelest in thine heart, and art sure, that
all is false which they say, yet thou couldest not solve
their subtle riddles." (Preface to the Pentateuch.)

During his residence at Little Sodbury, Tyndale
preached at College Green, Bristol, and in the villages
around. It is remarkable, as a sign of the times, that
there was no resident bishop to interfere with him. For
the bishop was a thousand miles off, in Italy. It is
worthy of notice that this very non-resident bishop
afterwards became the Pope who kept Wolsey from
attaining to that much coveted position. His name,
when Bishop of Worcester, was Julio di Medici, and
afterwards Clement VII. He lived at Rome, and never
saw England! Henry VIII. wanted the Popedom for
Wolsey, but Charles V. eventually secured it for his
nominee. In fact, from 1512, when Sylvester di Giglio

returned to Rome, to 1535, when Hugh Latimer was consecrated, there was no resident Bishop of Worcester. A foreigner once held seven hundred preferments at a time, and another time orders came from Rome that three hundred Italians were to be appointed to the first benefices that fell vacant. So Dr. Parker, the Chancellor, did the bishop's work for him, being a violent bigot.

CHAPTER IV

TYNDALE GOES TO LONDON, AND THEN LEAVES ENGLAND FOR EVER

"Nunquam periclum sine periclo vincitur."

THUS, at length, not finding the quiet and liberty which he had looked for in a Gloucestershire manor house, in 1524 Tyndale went up to London, and tried to get into the service of the Bishop of London, but in vain. "Room enough," he says, "there was in my Lord's house for belly-cheer, but none to translate the New Testament." The Bishop was Tunstall, a courtly scholar, but no Reformer,* though friendly with Erasmus and More.

"To place and power, all public spirit tends,
In place and power all public spirit ends."

Tyndale said afterwards that Erasmus had a tongue which made of little gnats great elephants, if any one favoured him. His stay in London was not in vain, however, in view of the life-work God was calling him to. He marked the course of the world; heard the preachers, whom he calls praters; and beheld the pomp of the prelates; and how they endeavoured to set unity and peace in the world, "themselves walking in darkness all the time." He wanted nothing more than a yearly income of ten pounds for his subsistence, and some post in which he might preach the Word of God and teach children. Soon after his arrival, a wealthy and bene-

---

* Afterwards Tyndale had reason to call him "that still Saturn, the imaginer of all mischief."

OLD ST. DUNSTAN'S, WHERE TYNDALE PREACHED.

volent citizen, Humphrey Monmouth by name, who was a Reformer in his principles, and had bestowed exhibitions in the Universities, received Tyndale under his roof, and engaged to supply him with all that was necessary. He heard him preach several times at St. Dunstan's. Humphrey Monmouth was sent to the Tower in May 1528, for reading "heretical books." But better times came, and he was made Alderman and Under-Sheriff of London. He was a draper, be it said, to the honour of the fraternity. Fryth also became Tyndale's friend while he was in London. He was not unmolested, however; and after six months of hard labour in God's word, he left our shores for a safer retreat somewhere abroad.

From his boyhood, Tyndale tells us, he had felt himself called to the work which he had now begun. So, finding that there was no room, not only in the bishop's palace, but in all England to translate the New Testament, he was determined to go where there was. There can be very little doubt that the first English New Testament was produced at far-famed Wittenberg. Tyndale landed at Hamburg, but there was not a solitary printer there then, and the fame of Luther would be sure to attract such a man. All the contemporaneous evidence agrees, and it is almost certain that he spent his first continental year where Luther was now a married man and could easily receive his friends. On the way he would find evidences of the Reformation right and left, convents abandoned, the mass giving place to the Lord's Supper, and the people freely permitted to read the Scriptures in their own tongue. He soon learnt German, and would be amongst the crowd in the University Church listening to the intrepid Reformer. I was there some years ago, and it was encouraging to be told by the verger that the congregations were as large to-day as when Luther preached. It is not unlikely also that such a man as Tyndale would get into private intercourse with Luther, and be inspired by some of his table talk. He had just translated the Bible himself into the German vernacular, and thrown his inkstand at the devil for interfering with him!

His helper, during this memorable year, was Friar Roye, as he could get none better, and it was necessary to have some secretary or amanuensis. What they went

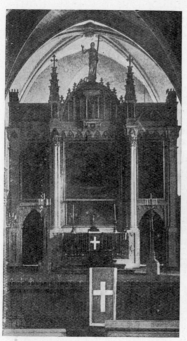

STATE CHURCH, WITTENBERG, IN THE CONFESSIONAL OF WHICH LUTHER WAS TOLD ABOUT TETZEL.

STATE CHURCH, WITTENBERG, WHERE MANY OF LUTHER'S SERMONS WERE PREACHED.

to work with was the third edition of Erasmus's New Testament in Greek, with its Latin Version. This was the foundation, and they had also the Vulgate, Luther's German translation, and such grammars and lexicons as the age furnished.

Roye had been at Cambridge, and then a friar at

WITTENBERG UNIVERSITY.

LUTHER'S ROOMS WERE TO THE RIGHT OF THE TOWER, ON THE FIRST FLOOR.

3

Greenwich, when his eyes were opened to the true
character of Popery. He was not, however, one of the
brightest champions of the new faith ; and though Tyndale
used him, no friendship was formed between them.
Tyndale's account of him is that, as long as he had no
money, he could rule him ; but, as soon as he got money,

CASTLE CHURCH, WITTENBERG.

" he became like himself again." He says they compared
texts together, which he could not do alone, and then he
bade him farewell " for our two lives, and, as men say, a
day longer."

It certainly seems suitable that the first English New
Testament should have been produced at Wittenberg,
" the cradle of the Reformation." We shall see directly

that it was printed at Worms, where the mighty Diet had been only four years before, so its connection with two of the chief scenes of the Reformation is sufficiently strong. The Castle Church at Wittenberg was restored in 1892, and contains the tombs of Luther, Melanchthon, Frederick the Wise, and John the Steadfast. On

THE VERITABLE DOOR OF THE THESES.

its old doors, now replaced, Luther nailed his ninety-five theses, and there is a tree outside the Elster Gate where he burned the Papal Bull. There is a fine bronze statue to " the solitary monk that shook the world," by Schadow, in the market-place, but neither at Wittenberg nor Worms is there any trace of Tyndale, whose quiet work, however, was just as enduring.

However, though translated, the first New Testament was not printed at Wittenberg. It was too strongly identified with books that would be called heretical, and Tyndale moved on to Cologne, a large commercial shipping centre. The Romanist policy everywhere was like that of the Philistines, who would allow no smith in Israel, lest the Hebrews should make them swords or spears.* But in such a Romanist city, a printer of "heresies" would scarcely be suspected. Nevertheless, it was whilst at Cologne, where Tyndale arrived in June 1525, that

CASTLE CHURCH, WITTENBERG, WHERE THE THESES WERE NAILED
UP, AND LUTHER AND MELANCHTHON ARE BURIED.

Cochlæus, best known for his ferocious attacks on Luther, interrupted the printing of the sheets, getting an order from the Senate, which nearly spoilt the labours of many patient months. Later on, this man (whose real name was John Dobneck) entered on this very translation controversy, printing a letter to James V. of Scotland, as to whether it was expedient for laymen to read the Scriptures. It is to this letter chiefly that we owe the minute account of the whole of the transactions at this

* *Scripture the Illustrator*, Bowes.

time, of which Cochlæus was not a little proud.* The printing was being executed by Peter Quentel; and Cochlæus made some of his workmen drunk, that he might get the secret out of them. It was through the interest taken in the matter by Rinck, a patrician of Cologne, to whom Cochlæus disclosed what he had discovered, that the order of the Senate was given which put an end to the printing for the present.

There were many well-known printers in such a city as Cologne, Ulric Zell, having been the first, in 1466. It is probable, however, that Quentel was amongst the foremost of his day, and Cologne is likely to have been chosen by Tyndale as a good place to remain undiscovered in, being a city of great importance, the birthplace of Rembrandt, the capital of the Duchy, and a centre of commerce. It is worthy of note that the first instances of books printed with imprimaturs, or Romish official permissions, are two printed in this same city of Cologne in 1479, one of them being a Latin Bible.

It is perhaps rather strange, however, that Tyndale should have chosen a place like Cologne to commence his printing operations in, considering how fierce was the *odium theologicum* of that time, unless it was that he thought he would be hid. One Doctor at this time hung up the portrait of Erasmus in his study, that he might be able at any moment to spit in his face!

With Roye as his companion, Tyndale now took the quarto sheets already printed, as far as the printer's signature "к," and fled, by a ship going up the Rhine, to that famous Worms, where Luther had taken his stand at the Diet only four years previously. It is almost a wonder he did not go to Antwerp, not far away, and then the headquarters of Bible printing. Here no fewer than thirteen editions of the Bible and twenty-four of the New Testament, in Dutch or Flemish, were printed

---

* Roye said of Cochlæus :

> "A little, praty, foolish poade ;
> But, although his stature be small,
> Yet men say he lacketh no gall ;
> More venomous than any toad."

TYNDALE'S WATER-WAY, COBLENTZ.

during the first part of the sixteenth century; besides
many others in various languages.

Worms was chosen, however, most likely, for more
than one reason. Its strong Lutheran feeling; its being
straight up the Rhine; and, perhaps, the fact of Schoeffer
being there, may have influenced Tyndale. The modern
traveller will remember that he had thus to sail up the
loveliest part of the Rhine. But there were no gay steamers
crowded with tourists then ; and we can only guess at
the effect produced on his mind by the seven mountains,
the castle-crowned heights, and the innumerable fables

TYNDALE'S WATER-WAY, EHRENBREITZTEIN.

and traditions which haunt the famous river. With his
work interrupted in the middle, and so far a failure, it is
not likely that Tyndale would be in the mood to make
many inquiries. But we may imagine him, many a time,
led out in prayer, in the lovely solitudes through which
he would pass; and pacing, it may be, a heavy barge,
similar to those which the traveller now frequently sees
slowly working their way against the strong deep current.

The associations of the towns through which Tyndale
passed, however, would not be lost upon him. At
Cologne, which he now quitted, there had been, only a few

years back, a disturbance which had thrown into bold relief the two parties which now divided the Church. Reuchlin, by whom the study of classical literature and Hebrew was greatly promoted, had been involved in a quarrel with a Jew of Cologne, called Pfefferkorn, who, at the age of fifty, had made a profession of Christianity. Pfefferkorn published some works for the purpose of converting his Jewish brethren, but without much success. He then petitioned the Emperor Maximilian that all Jewish books, except the Bible, might be destroyed. It was suggested to the Emperor that Reuchlin should be consulted; and, accordingly, he gave his judgment in an argumentative treatise. In this he distinguished the books of the Jews into seven classes, and affirmed that amongst the lighter sort only was there anything in mockery of the Christian religion, and that the rest might profitably be studied. Pfefferkorn at once assailed Reuchlin, in a book called the *Hand-glass*; to which Reuchlin rejoined in one entitled the *Eye-glass*, in which he convicted his adversary of twenty-four untruths. Then came the Dominican Monks upon the scene, who made Reuchlin apologise for some of his language, though he would retract nothing. The end of it was that Sickingen, a noble who had strongly espoused Reuchlin's cause, and that of the Reformation generally, threatened that, unless the payment of damages was made within a month, he would lay waste the territory of Cologne. In consequence of this, the Inquisitor made his payment; and Reuchlin was undisturbed till the day of his death. All this, full of the lights and shadows of the Reformation period, had occurred immediately before Tyndale's residence in Cologne.

He would not forget either that, at the University of Cologne, John Wessel, styled by his admirers " the light of the world," and by his opponents "the master of contradictions," was educated. Of his works, Luther says : " If I had read them earlier, my enemies might have thought that I derived everything from him, so much does the spirit of the two agree." Being asked by the Pope, who had known him in early life, to choose some gift, Wessel selected a Bible in the original tongues, from the Vatican Library. When the Pope expressed his wonder that he had not selected a bishopric, or some valuable benefice, Wessel replied that he did not need any such things.

Passing Oberwessel, the birthplace of John Richrath, Tyndale would again be reminded that there was nothing very modern about his views. For Richrath, like Luther, had been disgusted by the preaching of Indulgences; so that he wrote, not only against the grosser abuses of the system, but the whole principle of it.

Perhaps the reader would like to have a sample or two of these far-famed Indulgences. The following is in the *Hours after the Use of Sarum*, printed at Paris, in 1526 : "To all that be in a state of grace, that devoutly say this prayer (fol. 38) before the Blessed Lady of Pity; she will show them her Blessed Visage, and warn them the day and hour of their death." Again, "John the Third, Pope of Rome, at the request of the people of England, hath granted to all them that devoutly say this prayer, before the image of our Lord crucified, as many days of pardon as there are wounds in the body of our Lord, in the time of His bitter passion, the which were 5465."*

Richrath attained great popularity as a preacher, at Worms. But he did not avoid the extravagances into which men of his class so easily fall. He once said that, if Peter instituted fasting, it was with a view to getting a better market for his fish ! His writings were burned, and he was sent to the Convent of Augustinian Friars at Maintz (Mayence), where he soon afterwards died.

Yes ! Maintz, the home of printing in Germany, would be Tyndale's last stopping-place. And, no doubt, his purpose would be strengthened, as he reflected how the printing presses here had groaned under German Bibles long enough; whilst his own country was destitute of one single printed English Bible. Fourteen complete editions

* The prayers are in Latin (Antiquarian Repository, London, 1807).

in High German, and four in Low, had been issued; though not without opposition. Berthold, Archbishop of Maintz, in 1486, denounced the publishing of any books not allowed by four Doctors, especially the Bible. A Bull of Alexander VI., in 1501, recited that many pernicious books had been published in various parts, especially in the Provinces of Cologne, Maintz, Treves, and Magdeburg; and forbidding all printers to publish any books, without the licence of the archbishops and their officials. " Scarabaeus aquitam querit" — the beetle destroyed the eggs of the eagle, in revenge for an injury; so said Erasmus, in his adages. For a time, however, the nobility gave some influence to the new reforming ideas. Both in Germany and in France they were the first to embrace them, and the first to desert them.

Of course in England the Scriptures had been practically forbidden to the people. Not theoretically, as Mr. Demaus points out. Men were not forbidden to translate the Scriptures, but only " of their own authority." So said the Constitution passed at Oxford in 1408, but that was more than a century before, and the bishops had never provided the reliable text. Instead of that, they had been unrelenting in their severity towards all who dared to read Wycliff's version, which was the only one. They took no steps whatever to supersede that, which they found fault with, by a better.

CHAPTER V

"Often shall we find
The sharded beetle in a safer hold,
Than is the full-winged eagle."

CYMBELINE.

THERE can be no reasonable doubt that it was to Worms that Tyndale went; a piece of gossip, harmlessly exaggerated, identifying him there in 1526. Spalatin, who was with the Elector of Saxony at Spires, twenty miles off, notes in his diary: " On the Saturday, the morrow of St. Lawrence (August 10th, 1526), our Prince, the Elector of Saxony, then at the Diet of Spires, having heard a sermon at the residence of the Landgrave of Hesse, returned to his house. Buschius told us at supper that, at Worms, six thousand copies of the New Testament were printed in English. This work was translated by an Englishman, who was staying there, with two of his countrymen ; and who was so learned in seven languages (Hebrew, Greek, Latin, Italian, Spanish, English, and French) that, whichever he spoke, you would think it his native tongue. The English, indeed, have such a desire for the Gospel, although the king dislikes and opposes it, that they say they would buy a New Testament, even if each copy cost 100,000 pieces of money."

With regard to the number said to be printed, namely, 6000, it is probable that it is to be divided between the quarto edition begun at Cologne, and the octavo edition printed entirely at Worms. Perhaps Tyndale found a difficulty in matching the Cologne printer's type, and so proceeded with a fresh octavo edition. The quarto sheets, up to the printer's signature " K," may have been sent to England, to be completed there. But it is doubtful whether this edition was ever finished. The solitary fragment in the British Museum was only found in 1834; though libraries are being ransacked more than ever.

At any rate, the octavo edition was produced first; and it was quickly issued, without notes, from Peter Schoeffer's press. Thus the first printed English New Testament saw the light in the ancient and historic city of Worms; to which, only four years before, Luther had been summoned, and where he went, though, as he said, he should find as many devils as there were tiles on the housetops. I have tried to find the exact spot in Worms where Tyndale had his Testament printed, the first of an illustrious line. I failed; but it is probably still there, most of the houses being ancient, and very much as Luther and Tyndale saw them. If the hypothetical number of devils had been reached, it would have been enormous, the houses having usually long sloping roofs, such as delighted Mr. Ruskin.

Schoeffer, the printer, on becoming a Lutheran, had found it desirable to leave Maintz and settle at Worms, which he did in 1512. He was the son of the famous associate of Faust and Gutenberg, the original printers, whose statues adorn the Frankfort market-place. Works issuing from his press, about the same time, have similar type, capital letters, length and number of lines in a page, water-mark, and wood-cuts; as Mr. Fry has shown, after thorough investigation.

Tyndale translated chiefly from the Greek original, and not from the Vulgate, as was the case with preceding versions; and the one thing he aimed at, above all, was accuracy of text. He says, in a letter to his friend Fryth : " I call God to record, against the day we shall appear before the Lord Jesus, to give a reckoning of our doings, that I never altered one syllable of God's word, against my conscience; nor would do, this day, if all that is in the earth, whether it be honour, pleasure, or riches, might be given me." So far was he from seeking personal fame or gain, that he promised Henry VIII. that, if he would have the bare text of Scripture given to the people, by whomsoever translated, he would never write more. God had marked him out for the work, however; and no one now grudges him the highest praise as a translator. He consulted the Vulgate, the Latin translation of Erasmus, and Luther's German Bible. He was not, however, otherwise aided by Luther, as has been thought. The two men were, indeed, prosecuting the same labour, at the same era, and in the same thoroughgoing way. Luther's care to produce an exact translation was so great that, finding some difficulty in expressing the different parts of animals which are treated of in the sacrificial laws, he got butchers to dress sheep before him, that he might see the parts referred to, and be sure of the proper German names for them.*

Whether Tyndale thoroughly knew German at this time is doubtful; and the idea of there being a number of Germanisms in our present version in consequence is probably erroneous. There are many such expressions as —" So ordain I in all the churches "; " to the weak became I "; " of the Jews five times received I "; but this form of expression is equally common in the early Anglo-Saxon and English.†

Tyndale was a very good Greek scholar, however, and his instincts, as a Reformer, would lead him to rely principally on this. He took a translation of one of the orations of Isocrates, when he went to see the Bishop of London, as a sample of his powers; and no doubt the language, practically rediscovered, would have a great

---

* Mathesius.
† *e.g.* Chaucer's *Knight's Tale.*
        " Her eyen cast she full lowe adowne."
        " And lyke a lyon loked he aboute."
        " Full hye upon a chare of golde stode he."
In Chaucer's prose also the same order is frequently observed. " She may have mercy, this mote I will " (*Parson's Tale*).
   The Anglo-Saxon Scriptures also have : " Tha genan he an ribb of his siden." The fact is, Tyndale frequently comes nearer to the original than either Luther, the Vulgate, or the LXX. (H. Walker, B.D., Letter to Bishop of Peterborough, 1828).

charm for him.   He answers the old objection, that the
Scripture makes men heretics, in a characteristic way, in
a note on 1 John—"Because their darkness cannot
comprehend the light of the Scripture, they turn it into
blind riddles, and read it without understanding, as laymen do our Lady's Matins, or, as it were, Merlin's
prophecies.   Their minds are ever upon their heresies,
and when they come to a place that soundeth like, there
they rest, and ring out wonderful expositions to establish
their heresies withal.   Like the tale of the boy who

EDITION OF NEW TESTAMENT BEGUN AT COLOGNE.

would fain have eaten of the pasty of lampreys, but durst
not, until the bells seemed to sing unto him—'Sit down,
Jack boy, and eat of the lampreys!' to establish his
wavering conscience."

There is only a fragment of the first quarto edition
known to exist; and it has been discovered during the
present century, as we have said, bound up with another
volume.   Of the first octavo edition there remain but
two copies.   A further revision of the New Testament,
however, was published in 1534, much superior to those

which had preceded it; and from this Tyndale's labours

WORMS NEW TESTAMENT,
PRINTED BY SCHOEFFER, 1525, WITHOUT GLOSSES OR PROLOGUE.

TYNDALE'S PENTATEUCH, WITH WOODCUTS.

may best be judged. There is very little fault, however,
to be fairly found with his first edition. Dr. Geddes has

4

I haue here translated (brethern and susters moost dere and tenderly beloued in Christ) the newe Testament for youre spirituall edyfyinge / consolacion / and solas: Exhortynge instantly and besechynge those that are better sene in the tonge then y / and that haue hyer gyftes of grace to interpret the sence of the scripture / and meanynge of the sprite / then y / to consydre and pondre my laboure / and that with the spyrite of mekenes. And yf they perceyue in eny places that y haue not attayned the very sence of the tonge / or meanynge of the scripture / or haue not geuen the right englysshe worde / that they put to there handes to amende it / rememberynge that so is there duetie to doo. For we haue not receyued the gyftes of god for oure selues only / or for to hyde them: but for to bestowe them vnto the honouringe of god and christ / and edyfyinge of the congregacion / wchich is the body of christ.

The causes that moved me to translate / y thought better that other shulde ymagion / then that y shulde rehearce them. More over y supposed yt superfluous / for who ys so blynde to axe why lyght shulde be shewed to them that walke in dercknes / where they cannot but stomble / and where to stomble ys the daynger of eternall dampnacion / other so despyghtfull that he wolde enuye eny man (y speake nott his brother) so necessary a thinge / or so bedlem madde to affyrme that good is the naturall cause of ynell / and derknes to procede oute of lyght / and that lyinge shulde be grounded in trougth and veryte / and nott rather clene contrary / that lyght destroyeth dercknes / and veritie reproveth all manner lyinge.

A ij

ST. MATTHEW.

51

The First Chapter.

Tys is the bo=
ke off the generacion off
Jhesus christ the sonne of Da=
vid/the sone also of Abraham.
Abraham begat Isaac:
Isaac begat Jacob:
Jacob begat Judas and hys
brethren:
Judas begat phares and zara
off thamar:
Phares begat Esrom:
Esrom begat Aram:
Aram begat Aminadab:
Aminadab begat Naasson:
Naasson begat Salmon:
Salmon begat Boos of Rahab:
Boos begat Obed of Ruth:
Obed begat Jesse:
Jesse begat David the krnge:
David the kynge begat Solomõ/of het that
was the wyfe of Vry:
Solomon begat Roboam:
Roboam begat Abia:
Abia begat Asa:
Asa begat Josaphat:
Josaphat begat Joram:
Joram begat Osias:
Osias begat Joatham:
Joatham begat Achas:
Achas begat Ezechias:

FACSIMILE OF FIRST CHAPTER OF FIRST ENGLISH NEW TESTAMENT EVER
PRINTED. P. QUENTEL'S QUARTO, COLOGNE, 1525. THE FRAGMENT
PRESERVED ONLY GOES AS FAR AS THE APPROPRIATE VERSE,
"FRIEND, HOW CAMEST THOU IN HITHERWARD!"—Matt. xxii. 12.

Ezechias begat Manasses:

Manasses begat Amon:

Amon begat Josias:

Josias begat Jechonias and hys brethren abs oute the tyme of the captivete of Babilon.

After they wer ledd captive to Babilon/Jes chonias begat Salathiel:

Salathiel begat Jorobabel:

Jorobabel begat Abiud:

Abiud begat Eliachim:

Eliachim begat Azor:

Azor begat Sadoc:

Sadoc begat Achin:

Achin begat Eliud:

Eliud begat Eleasar:

Eleasar begat Matthan:

Matthan begat Jacob:

Jacob begat Joseph the husbãde off Mary/of whome was boren that Jhesus which is called Christ.

All the generacions from Abrahã to David ar fowrtene generaciõs. And from David vns to the captivete of Babilon/are fowrtene genes racions. And from the captivete of Babilõ vns to Christ/are also fowrtene generacions.

The byrthe off Christe was on thys wys se/When hys mother mary was maryed vnto Joseph/before they cam to dwell togeoder/she was founde with chylde by the holy goost. Thẽ her husbande Joseph beinge a parfect man/ãd loth to defame her/was mynded to put her aws aye seeretly. Whill he thus thought/behold the ãgell of the lord apeted vnto hĩ in slepe saige: Jo

margin notes:
4 Regiem 2c.

1 Esdre 2.

Luce primo

said that, "although it is far from a perfect translation, yet few first translations will be found preferable to it. It is astonishing how little obsolete the language of it is, even at this day. And, in point of perspicuity and noble simplicity, propriety of idiom, and purity of style, no English version has yet surpassed it."

For Tyndale's notes, indeed, he was largely indebted to Luther, as might be expected. But in these also he is original, and differs from Luther on a variety of points, notably in relation to St. James's Epistle, and that to the Hebrews. He was never weary of altering, where he thought he could mend. And a host of minute changes are found, when one edition is compared with another. But, throughout, he went upon general principles which have been accepted ever since. The Bible was to be a book for the people, and not for the scholar merely. It was thus often highly vernacular; as, for instance, "When ye pray, babble not much." On "shake off the dust of your feet," he writes: "That is, see that ye take nothing of them; insomuch that ye shake off the very dust from your shoes, that they may know how ye sought, not your own profit, but their health." On "Hosanna," he says: "Hosanna! is as much as to say Och, helppe! or, Och! give good luck, and health!" Tyndale's last Testament, in 1535, was published without notes; ending thus as he began.

Erasmus's work was, doubtless, of the greatest assistance. It has already been referred to, but we must spend a little longer time upon it. His translation and paraphrase of the New Testament was a production suitable to his genius and scholarship; though it was, unfortunately, too hurried. It was published in 1516, by Froben, of Basle, a well-known printer of the time, to whose instigation the work was largely due. It contained, in two columns, side by side, the original Greek, and a new Latin translation of his own; thus laying the foundation for Tyndale's work, or that of any translator into the vernacular. In the Preface, he asks why it seems indecent for any one to read or pronounce the gospel in that tongue wherein he

Hys ys the boke of the generaciō of Jesus Christ the sonne of David/The sonne also of Abra ☧Abraham begatt Isaac: [ħā.

Isaac begatt Jacob:

Jacob begatt Judas and hys brethren:

Judas begat Phares: [(thren:

and Zaram of thamar:

Phares begatt Esrom:

Esrom begatt Aram:

Aram begatt Aminadab:

Aminadab begatt naassan:

Naasson begatt Salmon:

Salmon begatt boos of rahab:

Boos begatt obed of ruth:

Obed begatt Jesse:

Jesse begatt david the kynge:

☧David the kynge begatt Solomon/of her that was the (wyfe of vry:

Solomon begat roboam:

Roboam begatt Abia:

Abia begatt asa:

Asa begatt iosaphat:

Josaphat begatt Joram:

Joram begatt Osias:

Osias begatt Joatham:

Joatham begatt Achas:

Achas begatt Ezechias:

Ezechias begatt Manasses:

Manasses begatt Amon:

Amon begatt Josias:

Josias begatt Jechonias and his brethren about the tyme of the captivite of babilon

☧After they were led captive to babilon / Jechonias begatt

*Abraham and David are fyrst rehearsld/ because that christe was chefly promysed vnto them.

Saynet mathew leveth out certeyne generacions/ z describeth Christes linage from solomō/after the lawe of Moses/ but Lucas descrībeth it accordyng to nature/frō nathan solomōs brother. For the lawe calleth them a mannes childrē which his broder begatt of his wyfe lefte behynde hym after his des the.deu.xxv.c.

FACSIMILE OF NEW TESTAMENT COMMENCED AND FINISHED
AT WORMS, 1525.

BAPTIST LIBRARY, AT BRISTOL.

was born?　"To me," he says, "it appears more indecent, or rather ridiculous, that ignorant men and young women, like parrots, mutter their Psalms and the Lord's Prayer in Latin, when they do not understand what they say, or the meaning of the noise they make."

Froben was one of the most learned men of the Basle University, and was the first of the German printers to bring the art to any perfection; the early printing being full of mistakes. He put up his proofs for public inspection, and gave a reward to any one discovering an error.

But although Erasmus's famous work was printed at Basle, its continental character almost ends there. At least, it was largely the work of his residence in England. He had the assistance of Englishmen in the examination of the manuscripts required; and English patrons lent that encouragement to the work which was needed, both in funds and influence. Specially was he indebted to Archbishop Warham and Lord Mountjoy. Many of the bishops also patronised the work, and spoke of it in high terms. It was, indeed, a bold step to take, to overthrow the authority of the Vulgate; and to show that some of the popular belief was founded on nothing but a misapprehension of the sacred text. Erasmus explained the text just as he would have explained any classic author, according to the best scholarship and science of the age; separating the spurious from the genuine; scattering to the winds all rules resting merely on authority, and replacing them by such as philology and history furnished. The interest taken in the work was widespread, owing largely to the fame of its author. And it was highly praised; one of the bishops declaring that it was worth more to him than ten commentaries.

Still, all was too hastily done, and the ill effects of the haste are to be recognised in our Authorised Version of to-day. The splendid edition of Cardinal Ximenes was soon to make its appearance; and Froben wished to publish the translation of Erasmus first, as he did. It was really a race, to anticipate the *Complutensian*

To the Reder.

Geve diligence Reder (I exhorte the) that thou come with a pure mynde / and as the scripture sayth with a syngle eye / vnto the wordes of health / ãd of eternall lyfe: by the which (if we repent ãd beleve them) we are borne a newe / created a fresshe / ãd enioye the frutes off the bloud of Christ. Whiche bloud cryeth not for vengeaũce / as the bloud of Abel: but hath purchased lyfe / love / faveour / grace / blessynge / and whatsoever is promysed in the scriptures / to them that beleve and obeye God: and stondeth bitwene vs and wrathe / vengeaunce / cursse / and whatsoever the scripture threateneth agaynst the vnbelevers and disobedient / which resist / and consent not in their hertes to the lawe of god / that it is ryght / wholy / iuste / and ought soo to be.

Marke the playne ãd manyfest places of the scriptures / and in doutfull places / se thou adde no interpretaciõ contrary to them: but (as Paul sayth) let all be conformable ãd agreynge to the

Note the difference of the lawe ãd ſ fayth. of the gospell. The one axeth and requyreth / the wother pardoneth and forgeveth. The one threateneth / the wother promyseth all good thyngs to them that sett their trust in Christ only. The gospell signifieth gladde tydyngs / and is nothynge butt the promyses off good thynges. All is not gospell that is writtẽ i the gospell boke: For if the lawe were awaye / thou couldest not know what the gospell meante. Even as thou couldest not se pardon / favour / and grace excepte the lawe rebuked the / and declared vnto thy the sinne / my dede / and treaspase.

Repent and beleve the gospell as sayth Christ

TYNDALE'S "ADDRESS TO THE REDER."

in the fyrst of Marke. Applye all wayethe lawe
to thy dedes/ whether thou finde luste in the bot=
tom of thyne herte to the lawe warde: and soo sh=
alt thou no dout repent/ãd seale in the silfe acer=
tayne sorowe/ payne/ and grefe to thyne herte:
be cause thou canst nott with full luste do the de=
des off the lawe. Applye the gospell ∕ that is to
saye the promyses/ vnto the deservynge off Chri=
st/ and to the mercye of god and his trouth/ ãd
soo shalt thou nott despeare: butt shalt feale god
as a kynde ãd a mercifull father. And his sprete
shall dwell inthe/ and shall be stronge in the: ãd
the promises shalbe geve the at the last (though
not bÿ ãd by∕ lest thou shuldest forgett thy sylfe
and be negligent) and all threatenyngs shalbe
forgeven the for Christis blouddis sake∕ to whõ
cõmit thy silfe all togedder/ with out respect/ ot=
her of thy good dedes or of thy badde.

Them that are learned Christenly/ J beseche:
for as moche as J am sure∕ ãd my conscience be=
areth me recorde∕ that of a pure entent/ singily
and faythfully J have interpreted itt∕ as farre
forth as god gave me the gyfte of knowledge∕ ãd
vnderstondynge: that the rudnes off the worke
nowe at the fyrst tyme/ offende them not: but th=
at they consyder howe that J had no man to co=
unterfet nether was holpe with englysshe of eny
that had intetpreted the same∕ or soche lyke thige
i the scripture before tyme. Moreover/ evẽ very
necessitie ãd combraunce (God is recorde) abo=
ve strengthe/ which J will not rehearce∕ lest we
shulde seme to bost oure selves∕ caused that ma=
ny thynges are lackynge/ whiche necessaryly are

To the Reder.

requyred. Count it as a thynge not havynge his full shape/but as it were borne afore hys tyme/even as a thig begunne rather then fynneslhed. In tyme to come(yf god have apoynted vs there vnto)we will gyveit his full shape: and putt out yf ought be added superfluusly : and adde to yf ought be oversene thorowe negligence: and will enfoarce to brynge to compendeousnes / that which is nowe translated at the lengthe/ād to geve lyght where it is requyred / and to seke ī certayne places more proper englysshe / and with a table to expoūde the wordes which are nott cōmenly vsed/and shewe howe the scripture vseth many wordes/which are wother wyse vnderstonde of the cōmen people: ād to helpe with a declaracion where one tonge taketh nott another. And will endever oure selves/as it were to sethe it better/and to make it more apte for the weake stomakes: desyrynge them that are learned/and able/to remember their duetie/ and to helpe there vnto:and to bestowe vnto the edyfyīge of Christis body.(which is the cōgregacion of them that beleve)those gyftes whych they have receaved of god for the same purpose. The gr ace that cōmeth of Christ be with thē that love hym.

praye for vs.

Polyglott of Ximenes, as far as the popular New Testament was concerned. In consequence, the manuscripts used were of no special value; even the best that were accessible not being made much use of. Bishop Ellicott has said that, whilst to speculate on such a mysterious ordering of Providence may be unwise, it does seem hard to resist the conviction that the great devotion and industry shown, generation after generation, in the critical study of the New Testament, would never have been called forth but for these circumstances. The knowledge that a purer text was attainable than that dignified by the title of the Universally Received Text, has quickened scholars in their lifelong labours. The Codex Basiliensis was amongst the manuscripts at the service of Erasmus; one of the most ancient and valuable; but he made scarcely any use of it, because its readings were so different from the others! With a little trouble, a collation with the Vatican MS. might also have been made.*

One edition of this Testament succeeded another, each being an improvement, until the fourth, which may be looked upon as the mother edition of our own Authorised Version, and of the Textus Receptus. The first two editions amounted to 3300; and the whole were in circulation by 1522, the year when the *Complutensian Polyglott* was published. Subsequent editions showed traces of the influence of this latter work upon Erasmus.†

It is amusing to think of the alarm and opposition which even such a great scholar's work excited. "Henry, Bishop of Saynt Asse," was Bishop of St. Asaph, and one of the brutal commissaries who had to do with the martyrdom of Bilney. On the appearance of Erasmus's first Testament, he is said to have fallen on his knees to the king and queen, and implored them to put him down. His title was often contracted, as here, into St. Asse, and the contraction was not unsuitable in his case, for Standish

---

* *Revision of English Version*, C. J. Ellicott, D.D.
† Tregelles. Account of printed text.

The fyfth Chapter.

When he sawe the people / he wentop vnto a mountaine / and when he was sett / his disciples cam vnto him / and he opended his mouth / and taughtthem (sayinge: Blessed are the pore in sprete: for theris the kyngdom of heven. Blessed are they that morne: for they shalbe comforted. Blessed are the meke: for they shall inheret the erth. Blessed are they which hunger and thurst for rightewesnes: for they shalbe filled. Blessed are the mercyfull: for they shall obteyne mercy. Blessed are the pure in hert: for they shall se god. Blessed are the maynteyners of peace: for they shalbe called the chyldren of god. Blessed are they which suffre persecucion for rightewesnes sake: fo: theirs is the kyngdom of heven. Blessed are ye when men shall revyle you / and persecute you / and shall falsly saye all manner of evyll (sayings) agaynst you for my sake. Reioyce and be gladde / for greate is youre rewarde in heven. Fo: so persecuted they the prophetts which were before youre dayes.

All these dedes here rehearsed as to noriffhe peace / ro fhewe mercy / to suffre pleacució / and fo forth / may ke not a man hap pye and blessed / nether deserve the rewarde of theven: but declare and testisfe that we are happy and blessed and that we shall have grete pmocion i theven. and certifye thvs i oure herttes that we are goddes sonnes / t that the holy gost is in vs. for all good thynges are geven to vs frely of god for chrilles bloudes fake ad his merittes

TYNDALE'S NEW TESTAMENT, 1525.
(UNREDUCED; SIZE OF WHOLE PAGE, 7½" × 5½".)

—that was his proper name—was very ignorant and bigotted. Erasmus called him "Episcopus a Sancto Asino." According to Roye's satire, it was he who first informed Wolsey of the arrival of Tyndale's English Testament, and implored him to suppress it.

CHAPTER VI

TYNDALE HARD AT WORK, AND FIERCELY OPPOSED

"God, of His goodness, grudged not to die,
Man to deliver from deadly damnation,
Whose will is that we should know perfectly
What He here hath done for our salvation.
O cruel Caiaphas, full of crafty conspiration,
How durst thou give then false judgment
To burn God's Word, the Holy Testament!

The lewdness of living is loath to bear
Christ's Gospel to come into clear light;
Howbeit surely it is so spread far and near
That, for to let it, thou hast little might.
God hath opened our dark dimmed sight
Truly to perceive thy tyrannous intent
To burn God's Word, the Holy Testament."

ROYE.

PERHAPS we should dwell a little on the parallel work of Ximenes, before returning to Tyndale. Cardinal Francis Ximenes, Archbishop of Toledo, commenced a Polyglott in the year 1502; the work being partly intended to celebrate the birth of the heir to the throne of Castile, afterwards Charles V. Theologians did not generally desire anything of the kind, being satisfied with the Vulgate, which was sometimes compared to Christ crucified between two thieves; the original Hebrew being on one side, and the Septuagint on the other. The Vulgate had, of course, been corrected from time to time; two succeeding Popes earning doubtful honours in the matter. Nicholas de Lyra, a converted Jew, of Normandy, who flourished about 1320, had also corrected many passages, according to the true sense of the Hebrew text; though he never attempted an entire revision.

Ximenes set to work, and accomplished this, with a number of helpers. The Old Testament was completed some time before the New, which appeared in vol. iv. of the entire work, in Greek and Latin, with the date January 10th, 1514. The Polyglott was finished in the same year as Martin Luther fixed his theses to the Electoral Chapel at Wittenberg; all the manuscripts used, however, being modern. Complutum is the Latin name for Alcala, in Spain, where the cardinal had founded a University, and where his work was printed. The Polyglott never came into any general use, though it was a fine production for the age, and its originator must have been a superior man. Erasmus's New Testament found its way round into Spain while Cardinal Ximenes was yet living, and he repressed the remarks by which Stunica, his chief New Testament editor, sought to depreciate it. " I would that all might thus prophesy," he said; " produce what is better, if thou canst ; do not condemn the industry of another." He did not live, however, to see the completion of his great enterprise; the publication of the whole not taking place till 1522. The editors say that they consulted old manuscripts from the Vatican Library. But Bishop Marsh says that the New Testament agrees almost always with modern manuscripts. Though never widely used, the work has been published again by Plantin at Antwerp, and at Geneva.

Tyndale was clearly supported in his enterprise by wealthy men, though, who they were, has never been quite cleared up. We have no knowledge of his coming to possess any property of his own. And we know that he was first a tutor, and then under obligations to a London merchant for board and lodging. Yet, notwithstanding the fact that, when he landed on the Continent, in May 1524, he was a poor and utterly unknown man, within two years he had printed two large editions of the New Testament, involving a considerable expense. He had to defray his own expenses also, and those of his assistant; and travelling about was not done by modern cheap coupons, " with a reduction for ministers." Perhaps he was supported, and his editions made possible,

CARDINAL XIMENES.

by the Antwerp merchants, amongst others, to whom he afterwards became a sort of chaplain. It is certain that there was both a strong anti-Romish and an anti-Wolsey feeling; and many Englishmen on the Continent were prepared to pay something for the Reformation of their own land.

However, the English New Testament, in its printed form, saw the light at last. And now the question was how to get it into England? The King and the Church were both against it; though Wolsey was at first in favour of tolerating it.* Moreover, in those days, there were no shops in which it could be sold. Nevertheless, to England it went, through Holland, by way of Antwerp; and it was soon found in London, Oxford, Norwich, and many other cities. The country was crying out for both kinds of bread, and with the wheat, which was largely imported at this time, went hundreds of copies of the Word of God. The first Testaments, indeed, were in England before the famine broke out in 1527. Their importation would be facilitated, therefore, just when it was needed, after opposition was aroused.

About this time there was formed in London a society calling itself the Association of Christian Brothers, and composed chiefly of poor men, with a very few of the clergy. Its agents perambulated the country, selling Testaments and tracts in the Universities and towns, and enrolling such persons as dared to belong to such a Society. The price of a Testament was half a crown, though the Dutch booksellers soon issued them for thirteen pence. The half-crown may be appreciated by a reference to the prices of other things in Henry VIII.'s reign. Hay was five shillings a load; beef and pork were a halfpenny a pound; and veal or mutton, three farthings. French wines were eightpence or a shilling a gallon. A mason was paid fourpence a day and his food, or sixpence without it. Women servants' wages were ten shillings a year, and four shillings for clothing. Perhaps the

---

* Afterwards he was soured by Roye's satire, "Rede me and be nott wrothe," which he wrongly attributed to Tyndale.

average multiple for the coins would be about seventeen in order to reach their present value.

The first notice of possession by any one dates from Colchester, and it is worth transcribing. John Pykas, a baker, confessed on March 7th, 1528, that "about two years ago, his mother, then dwelling in Bury St. Edmunds, sent for him, and moved him that he should not believe in the Sacraments of the Church; for that was not the right way. And then she delivered to this respondent a book of Paul's Epistles, in English, and bade him live after the way and manner of the said Epistles and Gospels, and not after the way the Church doth teach. Afterwards, when he heard that the said New Testament was forbidden, that no man should keep them, he delivered it, and the book of Paul's Epistles, to his mother again."

One of the most important of those who interested themselves in the sale of the Testaments was Richard Harman, a merchant of the English factory at Antwerp, who, with his wife, was imprisoned in 1528, but discharged the following year, and of whom we shall hear again. Another was Simon Fysche, author of *A Supplication for the Beggars*; which was answered at once by Sir Thomas More, who calls him a "dyspyteful person." When the persecution of 1528 arose he went abroad, but soon came back to London, and died there in 1530. Robert Necton also, whose brother was Sheriff of Norwich, in 1530, and who himself was in a good position, devoted himself to the work of colportage, merely from love of gospel principles. There can be no doubt that, through the labours of such men, the Testaments, though costing about £2 of our money, were sold with some rapidity.

One edition soon followed another, the quarto edition, which Cochlæus had delayed, being probably sold out, and also the first octavo one. An Antwerp printer, Christopher of Endoven, issued a third edition; and this was succeeded by a fourth. The Dutch printers printed 5000, in their two editions, which were smaller than Tyndale's. They engaged George Joye, an English refugee, to correct the sheets, which he did for fourteen shillings, but very faultily.

THE BURNING OF TYNDALE'S TESTAMENTS.

Of course, the reigning authorities took alarm at all this. As Southey says: "The Romanists knew perfectly well how little some of their practices were supported by Scripture; and that if the ark of the covenant was admitted, Dagon must fall." * Or, as Latimer said, in his plain way: "Where the devil is resident, and has his plough going, then away with books, and up with candles; away with Bibles, and up with beads; away with the light of the gospel, and up with the light of candles; yea, at noonday." Plutarch tells us of a painter, who, having painted a cock unskilfully, chased away the cocks out of the town, that the imperfection of his art might not appear; and it is well substantiated, that Warham, Archbishop of Canterbury, bought up either the first or a very early edition, and then levied a charge on each of the bishops; the sum expended being £66, 9s. 4d. His mandate is dated November 3rd, 1526, and directs that all copies of Tyndale's Testament shall be burned. A letter from the Bishop of Norwich, dated June 1527, approving of the course adopted, and offering his share, is still extant.† Tunstall also, Bishop of London, two years later, bought up another edition, probably when coming through Antwerp, on his way back from the Treaty of Cambray. He sent out a prohibition, dated October 23rd, 1526, in which he calls the new books "pestiferous and most pernicious poison"; accuses the authors of seducing the simple people by their wicked and perverse interpretations; and threatens excommunication unless all such books are brought in. A merchant, called Packington, was employed in the business; and, on the authority of Hall's *Chronicle*, Tyndale rather facilitated the sale. For he was convinced of some faults in the edition, and was then engaged in purging it, but had no money to print a new one. Besides, he felt sure that the burning of God's word, which was what the bishop designed and carried out, would rouse indignation, and lead to wholesome inquiry. So the money was paid, and

* *Book of the Church*, Southey.
† *Original Letters*, Ellis, vol. ii. series iii.

the books were publicly burned at St. Paul's Cross.   Next
year, when a further edition was finished, many more
copies came to England.   A man named Constantine, on
being taken and brought before the Lord Chancellor, was
promised that no hurt should be done to him, if he would
say who encouraged and supported the printers at
Antwerp.   When he at once replied that the greatest
encouragement they had was from the Bishop of London,
who had bought up half the previous impression.*   So,
"thinking he had God by the toe, he had the devil by
the fist."

It was resolved, indeed, at headquarters to stamp out
Tyndale's translations.   And, with regard to the first
editions, the work was so thoroughly done, that, of the
quarto Cologne edition, only a small fragment is known
to exist; and, of the Worms octavo, only two copies
remain; one being in the Baptist College Library, Bristol,
and the other in that of St. Paul's.   But they might
as well have tried to keep back the Atlantic with a
broom, like Mrs. Partington, the multiplication of editions
and copies being very rapid.   Six editions of the New
Testament were printed between 1525 and 1530, three
of which were surreptitious, showing how great was the
demand.   The public burning of Testaments in May
1531 appears to have caused a temporary bar to their
publication.   But in 1534 there were no less than five
editions of the New Testament printed at Antwerp.   In
1535 there were four editions of the New Testament,
and one of the whole Bible, which we shall describe
later on.   In 1536 no less than ten editions of the New
Testament, and one of the Bible, were printed; while in
1537 there were two editions of the Bible.   In 1538
there were seven editions of the New Testament; in 1539
four of the New Testament, and four of the Bible; and in
1540 four of the Bible, with three of the New Testament.
Though not all cheap, they were eagerly bought.   And we
have the remarkable fact that, within seventeen years of

* Doré (*Old Bibles*) should not blame Tyndale for selling his Testaments, in order to produce better ones.

OLD ST. PAUL'S AND PAUL'S CROSS, WHERE TESTAMENTS
WERE BURNED.

Tyndale's first New Testament, there were thirty-nine editions of the New Testament, and fourteen of the whole Bible. So mightily grew the Word of God, and prevailed. Henry VIII. tried, indeed, to stop the exportation from Antwerp, but the merchants there found that Christopher Endhoven, a much respected citizen, was then printing these books, and they declined to regard them as heretical.

If all the prohibitions and burnings failed, it was not for the want of strong language. The 1530 prohibition was to be published by the preachers, who were to say to their congregations :—

"Wherefore you that have the books called . . . the New Testament in English of the translation that is now printed, detest them, abhor them, keep them not in your hands; and if by reading of them heretofore anything remains in your breast of that teaching, either forget it, or by information of the truth expel it. Forasmuch as the King's Highness, by the advice and deliberation of his council, and the argument of the great learned men, thinketh in his conscience that the divulging of this Scripture at this time, in the English tongue, should rather be to their further confusion and destruction than the edification of their souls ; it was thought there, to all and singular in that congregation,* that the King's Highness and the prelates, in so doing, and not suffering the Scripture to be divulged to the people, do well." Well done, King, Prelates, and Council, all and very singular. *Qui habitat in coelis, irredebit eos.*

* That is, the Council.

CHAPTER VII

THE TRUE CHARACTER OF TYNDALE'S WORK

" Then for the style, majestic and divine,
It speaks no less than God in every line."

DRYDEN.

WE have seen something of the character of the man engaged in this work, at the risk of his life; and we should expect that anything bearing his name would have the marks of honesty and patient diligence. But Tyndale's translation has more excellences than these. It is not, indeed, going too far when we repeat what has often been said before, and by authorities of eminence, that his work has given a character to all future translations; and, amongst them, to that which is generally acknowledged to be the best in any vernacular, our Authorised Version. Tyndale's knowledge of Greek was sufficient to enable him to produce a work not offensive to scholars of unprejudiced minds. And he caught the popular ear in his terms and phrases, without descending to vulgarity.

Plumptre, for instance, says: " All the exquisite grace and simplicity, which have endeared the Authorised Version to men of most opposite tempers and contrasted opinions, are due mainly to his clear-sighted truthfulness." And Bishop Ellicott, out of a host of others, has said: " Tyndale not only furnished the type of all succeeding versions, but bequeathed principles which will exercise a preservative influence over the Version of the English Bible, through every change or revision that may await it, until Scriptural revision shall be no more needed."

The only dissonant note is from Mr. Blunt, who is not

specially appreciative; and who adduces an argument against any further revision, from the fact that the English people have a vested right in the Authorised Version, as so much property.* *Ex uno disce omnes.*

The prologue is an altogether remarkable piece of writing, and shows what the mind of the man was full of, in days when the mint and anise and cummin were put in place of the weightier matters of the law. It is, in fact, a general description of true religion, based upon redemption through Jesus Christ. He distinguishes between a self-righteous man, who justifies himself with his outward deeds, a voluptuous man (called a sense-well man), and a true Christian. After speaking of the nature of faith, and its effects, he closes with such a description of the Christian as it is not easy to excel. "Faith," he says, "receiveth of God, and love bestoweth the same on his neighbour. A true Christian man believeth that heaven is his already, by Christ's purchasing; and, therefore, he loveth and worketh to honour God only, and to draw all things to God. A Christian man feeleth the working of the Holy Ghost in his soul; and, in all tribulation and adversities, feeleth God a merciful and loving Father."

It may surprise our readers to see how small indeed is the change made from Tyndale's translation, except in the spelling. Selecting a passage at random and modernising it, Tyndale reads, in Matt. xvi. 13–19, "When Jesus came into the coast of the city which is called Cæsarea Philippi, He asked His disciples, saying, 'Whom do men say that I, the Son of Man, am?' They said, 'Some say that Thou art John Baptist; some, Elias; some, Jeremiah, or one of the prophets.' He said unto them, 'But whom say ye that I am?' Simon Peter answered and said, 'Thou art Christ, the Son of the living God.' And Jesus answered and said unto him, 'Happy art thou, Simon, the Son of Jonas; for flesh and blood have not opened unto thee that, but my Father which is in heaven. And I say also unto thee, that thou art Peter, and upon this rock will I build my congregation, and the gates of hell shall

* *Plain Account of the English Bible*, J. H. Blunt, F.S.A.

not prevail against it.   And I will give unto thee the keys
of the kingdom of heaven, and whatsoever thou bindest
upon earth, it shall be bound in heaven; and whatsoever
thou loosest on earth, it shall be loosed in heaven.'"*

As a sample of the marginal notes also, we give the
one on this passage.   "Peter, in the Greek, signifieth a
stone, in the English.   This confession is the rock.   How
is Simon Barjona, or Simon, Jonas's son, called Peter?
Because of his confession.   Whosoever, then, this wise
confesseth Christ, the same is called Peter.   Now is
this confession come to all that are true Christians.   Then
is every Christian man and woman Peter.   Read Bede,
Augustine, and Jerome, of the manner of loosing and
binding ; and note how Jerome checketh the presumption
of the Pharisees in his time, which yet had not such
monstrous interpretations as our new gods have feigned.
Read the annotations of Erasmus.   It was not for naught
Christ bade us beware of the leaven of the Pharisees.
Nothing is so sweet, but they make it sour, with their
traditions.   The Gospel, that joyful tidings, is now
bitterer than the old Law.   Christ's birch is heavier than
the yoke of Moses.   Our condition and estate is ten times
more grievous than was ever the Jews.   The Pharisees
have so leavened Christ's sweet bread."   As another
example of Tyndale's notes, take that on Matt. v. 22 :
"Raca is the hoarse sound in the throat, and betokeneth
all signs of wrath."

Yes, the contentions of those days were not about
trifles.   And it is well for us to remember that, three
times, at Gothic St. Paul's, which went before the present
structure, the Word of God was publicly burned.   The
first of these burnings was accompanied by a sermon from
Tunstall, at St. Paul's Cross opposite, in which he said that
Tyndale's Testament had 3000 errors.   Cardinal Wolsey
made one of his last appearances at the burning of Tyndale's
Testaments in 1530, when the people were solemnly
warned against the sin of reading what God had written,
and the Saviour had called men to search.   There is no

* From the Cologne quarto, interrupted by Cochlæus.

TYNDALE AT HIS WORK.

instance, however, of Wolsey's sending any one to the stake; and, to his immense ability, must be added his charity and extreme unwillingness to adopt harsh measures. His endeavour was, constantly, to win over the "heretic," and make his submission easy. It was not till the reins fell into the hands of Sir Thomas More that there was a change in this respect, which we shall dwell upon at some length. We will only say now that Sir Thomas More may be said to have lived to illustrate the necessary tendencies of Romanism, in an honest mind convinced of its truth; to show that the test of sincerity, in a man who professes to regard "orthodoxy" as an essential of salvation, is not the readiness to endure persecution, but the courage that will venture to inflict it. So says Froude.

Tyndale's brother John interested himself in the sale of the Testaments, with Thomas Patmore; and they were made to ride with their faces to the tails of their horses, having the heretical books hung about their cloaks, to the Standard at Cheapside, where they threw the books into the fire; being also heavily fined. Humphrey Monmouth, Tyndale's early friend, found a place in the Tower, and was almost ruined. Tewkesbury also, a similar man to Humphrey Monmouth, witnessed a good confession, and was tortured accordingly. When arraigned before the Bishop of London, and charged with reading the *Wicked Mammon,* a work of Tyndale's: "I find no fault in the book," he said, "but it is not my gospel. I have studied the Holy Scriptures these seventeen years; and, as a man sees the spots of his face in a glass, so by reading them I have learned the faults of my soul."

In the *Parable of the Wicked Mammon,* Tyndale says that Antichrist was not outward, but spiritual. He had been present in the times of the Old Testament, as in the New, and would be to the end. The book was condemned, of course; and then he published the *Obedience of a Christian Man.* In this he denounces the shutting up of the Bible thus: "That this threatening and forbidding the lay-people to read the Scripture is not for the love of

6

your souls (which they care for as the fox doth for the geese) is evident; inasmuch as they suffer you to read *Robin Hood, Bevis of Hampton, Hercules, Hector and Troilus,* with a thousand histories and fables of love and wantonness, and of ribaldry as filthy as heart can think."

He brings up a host of Romanist writings differing greatly from one another. They could not be piled up in any warehouse in London, and how should men know what to believe? His answer is, only by the Scriptures, and yet people are not permitted to have them.

They say the Scripture is so hard that it could never be understood but by the Doctors. This is to measure the meteyard by the cloth. Some of Origen's works are allowed, and some condemned for heresy, and how are they distinguished except by the Scriptures? Augustine knew more of Plato than the Scriptures at first, and when he came to know them he revoked part of what he had formerly written.

And as for its being necessary to know philosophy before we can understand God's Word, what philosophy is that? If it is Aristotle, his doctrine is that the world was without beginning, and shall be without end; that the first man never was, and the last never shall be; that God doth all of necessity, neither careth what we do, nor will ask any account of it. " Is it not a madness, then, to say that we cannot understand the Scripture without Aristotle! " Luther said once that if Aristotle had not been a man, he should have thought he was the devil.

As for Tyndale's writings causing insurrection, nothing could be further from the truth. It was of this last work that Henry VIII. said, " This book is for me and all kings to read." Luther had severely condemned the excesses of the Peasants' War in Germany, and Tyndale inculcated upon Englishmen their duty to their lawful Sovereign; though he justified a spiritual warfare against the usurped authority of the Pope. Evil rulers were a scourge of God. "Now, if the sick resist the razor, the scorching iron, and so forth, doth he not resist his own health?" His language was certainly strong in his

Practice of Prelates, published at Marburg; and he thinly disguises his references to Wolsey, under "Wolfsee." He erroneously laid on him and Longland, the Bishop of Lincoln, the blame of suggesting the divorce from Catherine of Aragon, and he had better have left the subject alone, as he did not understand it. After his *Obedience of a Christian Man*, Henry had tried to get him to return to England, but he quite dropped the idea when he read what he said about the divorce. It showed Tyndale's courage, however, and he only voiced the general feeling. Gairdner adds that Tyndale was a strong Imperialist, and disliked the divorce all the more because it was an injury to the emperor's aunt.*

* *History of the English Church.*

The pistle of paul
vnto Titus.

The fyrst Chapter.

Aul the servaunt of god
and an Apostle of Jesu Christ/
to preache the fayth of goddis e=
lecte/ and the knowledge off the
trueth/ which trueth is in servy=
nge god in hope of eternall lyfe
which lyfe god that cānotlye/ hath promysed be
fore the worlde began: but hath at the tyme ap=
oynted opēned his worde by preachynge/ which
preachynge is committed vnto me/ by the com=
aūdement of god oure saveoure.

To Titus his naturall sonne in the commen
fayth.

Grace mercie and peace from God the fath=
er/ and from the lorde Jesu Christ oure saveou=
re.

For this cause left J the in Creta/ that thou sh=
uldest performe that which was lackynge ād sh=
uldest ordeyne seniours in every citie as J apo=
ynted the. Jf eny be soche as no man can comp=
layne on/ the husbāde of one wyfe/ havynge fa=
ythfull children/ which are not sclandred off ro=
yote/ nether are disobediēt. For a bisshoppe mu=
st be soche as no man can complayne on/ as it be
commeth the minister off God. not stubborne
not angrye/ no dronkarde/ no fyghter/ not gevē

Ll v

Facsimile from the "Reproduction by
F.Fry 1862, of the First New Testament
in English by W^m. Tyndale (1525 or 26)"

The pistle of Paul

to filthy lucre: butt herberous / one that loveth
goodnes / of honest behaveout / righteous / holy
temperat / ād suche as cleveth vnto the true woz
de of doctryne / thatt he maye be able to exhozte
with wholsom learnynge / and to improve them
that saye agaynst it.

For there are many disobedient and talkers
off vanitie / and disceavers off myndes / namly
they off the circumcission / whose mouthes must
be stopped / which pervert whole houses / teach=
ynge thyngs which they ought nott / be cause off
filthy lucre. Won be ynge of them selves / which
was a poyet of their owne sayde: The Cretayns
are alwayes lyars / evyll beastes / and slowe be=
lies. This witnes is true / wherfore rebuke them
sharply / that they maye be sounde in the fayth /
and not takynge hede to sewes fables / and com=
maundments of men / which turne from the tru=
eth. Vnto the pure / are all thyngs pure: but vn=
to them that are defiled / ād vnbelevynge is no=
thynge pure: but even the very myndes and con=
sciences off them are defiled. They confesse that
they knowe god: but with dedes they denye hym
and are abhominable / and disobedient / ād vn=
to all good workes discommendable.

The. ij. Chapter.

Byt speake thou that which becōmeth whol
some learnynge: That the edler men be sob=
er / honest discrete / sounde in the fayth / in love ād
in pacience. And the elder weimen lyke wyse that
they be in soche rayment / as be cōmeth holynes /
not false accusars / not gevē to moche dzikynge /

but teachers of honest thyngs / that they nurter the yonge wemen for to love their husbādes / to love their children / to be of honest beh aveoure / chast / huswysly / good / and obedient vnto their aune husbandes / that the worde of god be not e͛ vyll spoken of. Yonge men lyk wyse exhorte that they be of honest manners.

Above all thyngs shewe thy silfe and insāple of good workes in the doctryne / shew vncorrup͛cion / honestie / and the wholsome worde which cānot be rebuked / that he which withstōdeth ma ye be ashamed / havynge no thīge in you that he maye dispraysе. The servaunts exhorte to be ob͛edient vnto their owne masters / and to pleasе in all thigs / not answerynge agayne / nether be pi͛ckers / but that they shewe all good faythfulnes that they maye do worshippe to the doctryne off god oure saveoure in all thynges. For the grace of god / that bryngeth health vnto all men / hath apered ād teacheth vs that we shulde denye vn͛godlynes / ād wordly lustes / ād that we shulde li ve honestly / righteously / and godly ī this preset worlde / lokīge for that blessed hope / ād glorious a perēge of the myghty god / ād of oure saviou͛re Jesu Christ: which gave hym silfe for vs / to rede me vs frō all vnrightewesnes / ād tō pourdge vs a peculiar peoplе vnto hī silfe fervētly gevе vnto good works. These thīgs speake / ād exhorte / ād rebuke / with all cōmaūdynge. Se that no man despise the. **The .iij. Chapter.**

WArne them that they submit them selves to ruele and power / to obey the officers / that they be prōpt vnto all good works / that they

speake evyll off no man / that they be no fyghte=
rs / but ſofte / ſhewynge all meknes vnto all men
For we ouré ſelves alſo were in tymes paſt / vn=
wyſe / diſobedient / deceaved / in daunger to lu=
ſtes / and to divers mannners off voluptuſnes /
livynge in maliciouſnes / and envie / full of hate
hatynge one another.

But after that the kyndnes and love of oure
ſaveoure to man warde apered / not of the ſedes
off rightewesnes which we wrought / but off his
mercie / he ſaved vs / by the fountayne of the ne=
we birth / and with the renuynge off the holy go=
oſt / which he ſhed on vs aboundantly / thorow
Jeſus Chriſt oure ſaveoure / that we once iuſti=
fied by his grace / ſhulde be heyres off eternall ly
fe / thorow hope. This is a true ſayinge.

Off theſe thyngs J wolde thou ſhuldeſt certi=
fie / that they which beleve God / myght be ſtod=
lous to go forwarde in goode workſ. Theſe thy=
ngſ are goode and proffetable vnto men. Foliſ=
ſhe queſtions / and genealogies / and brauling⸗
and ſtryfe aboute the lawe avoyde / for they are
vnproffetable / and ſuperfluus. A man that is
the auctor off ſectes / after the fyrſt and the ſeco=
nde amonicion avoyde / remembrynge that he
that is ſoche / is perverted / and ſynneth / even
damned by his awne iudgement.

When J ſhall ſende Artemas vnto the or Ti=
chicus be diligēt to come to me vnto Nichopolis
For J have determined there to wynter. Bryn=
ge Zenas the lawear and Apollos on their ior=
ney diligently / that nothynge be lackynge vnto
them. And let oures alſo learne to excell in goode
workes for neceſſarie uſes that they be not
unfruptefull.

CHAPTER VIII

"Corruptio optimi pessima."

ARGUMENT, however, was resorted to as well as force; and Sir Thomas More entered the lists against Tyndale, publishing a dialogue, which was soon answered. More said that he did not object to a vernacular translation, but it should be undertaken by men of Catholic minds, in times less rife with religious dissension, and should have the approval of the ecclesiastical authorities. Let us look in upon them at the fray, selecting what belongs to our subject.

More.—Christ said not the Holy Ghost shall write, but shall teach. Whatsoever the Church says, it is the Word of God, though it be not in Scripture.

Tyndale.—What! Christ and the Apostles not speaking of Scripture! These are written, says St. John, that ye might believe, and through belief have life.

More.—The Apostles have taught by mouth many things they did not write; because they should not come into the hands of the heathen, for mockery.

Tyndale.—I pray you, what thing more to be mocked by the heathen could they teach than the Resurrection? And that Christ was God and man, and died between two thieves? Yet all these things the Apostles wrote. Again, Purgatory, penance, satisfaction for sin, and praying to saints, are marvellous agreeable unto the superstition of the heathen people; so that they need not to abstain from writing of them, for fear lest the heathen should have mocked them.

In another place, Tyndale puts the Popish legends by the side of the Talmud. "As the Jews have set up a book of traditions, called Talmud, to destroy the sense of Scripture; unto which they give faith, and unto the Scripture none at all, be it never so plain; but say it cannot be understood, save by the Talmud; even so have ours set up their Duns, their Thomas, and a thousand like draff, to stablish their lies, through falsifying the Scripture; and say that it cannot be understood without them, be it never so plain. And if a man allege a holy Doctor against them, they glose him out, as they do the Scripture; or will not hear; or say the Church hath otherwise determined. They have also corrupted the Legends and Lives of nearly all the Saints. They have feigned false books, and put them forth; some in the name of St. Jerome, some in the name of St. Augustine, in the name of St. Cyprian, St. Dionyse, and other holy men; which are proved none of theirs, partly by the style and Latin, and partly by authentic stories."

More.—We must not examine the teaching of the Church by Scripture, but understand Scripture by means of what the Church says.

Tyndale.—What! does the air give light to the sun, or the sun to the air? God begat, with His own will, with the Word of Truth, says St. James. If he who begetteth is before him who is begotten, the Word is before the Church.

More.—The Romish Church, from which the Lutheran came out, was before them, and therefore is the right one.

Tyndale.—In like manner you may say that the Church of the Pharisees, when Christ and His Apostles came out, was before them, and therefore was the right Church.

More.—I marvel that you deny Purgatory, Sir William, unless it be a plain point with you, to go straight to hell.

Tyndale.—I know no other purging, but faith in the Cross of Christ. While you, for a groat, or a sixpence, buy some secret pills (indulgences), which you take to purge yourself of your sins.

More.—Faith, then, is your Purgatory. You say there is no need, therefore, of works ; a most immoral doctrine.

Tyndale.—It is faith alone that saves us; but not a bare faith. When a horse beareth the saddle, and a man thereon, we may well say that the horse only, and alone, beareth the saddle ; but we do not mean the saddle empty and no man thereon.

Three special words of Tyndale's More singled out for his vituperation ; congregation instead of church ; elder, for priest; and love, for charity. Tyndale answers him at length. With regard to church, he says that congregation is better, since the idea of church has come, under Popish influences, to be limited to its ministers. Thomas à Becket, for instance, died for the liberties and privileges of the Church, *i.e.* liberty to do all mischief unpunished by the secular arm. But what he always understands by the Church is "The Pope, Cardinals, Legates, Patriarchs, ... Friars, black, white, pied, grey, etc." And as for Ecclesia always being translated Church ; it is used three times in one chapter, the 19th of Acts, of a congregation of heathen people, with their Demetrius.

Think of Sir Thomas More, the most accomplished man of his time, becoming, under the influence of Popery, a Judge Jefferies ! He thirsted for the blood of those who differed from him in matters of faith, if he did not turn the screw with his own hands to torture them, and jest at his victim's sufferings. As Lord Chancellor he understood the rights of person and property. To the human mind only he would allow no liberty whatever. Why did he attack Tyndale's New Testament as ignorant, dishonest, and heretical ? Partly because, for ecclesiastical terms, Tyndale used others, as we have seen ; church was congregation, priest was elder; charity was love ; grace was favour ; penance was repentance ; and confession was knowledge (acknowledge). Sir Thomas More cast Bainham, a Reformer, into prison within his own house, and was commonly said to have whipped him at a tree in his garden, called the tree of truth. After which he sent him to be tortured on the rack at the Tower.

S.^R THO.^S MORE.

More was the first man who persuaded Henry VIII., publicly and personally, to imbrue his hands in the blood of his subjects on English ground, as Catherine Sinclair says. Oh yes, Wolsey was much milder, and it was a charge brought against him that "he was the impeacher and disturber of due and direct correction of heresies." He stood by Latimer against his own persecuting bishop.

It was a sign of the times that even Sir Thomas, considered then to be the greatest wit in England, had to ask, or did ask, permission to read Tyndale's works, with a view to replying to them. The permission was granted by Bishop Tunstall, who gave it him "forasmuch as he could play the Demosthenes." He played it. But Arber's criticism on his performance is a just one, when he says that the whole of More's well-meant efforts in the controversy are a distortion of the natural bent of his genius, leading him to a reckless vituperation of his opponents.*

It is painful to have to speak disparagingly of such a man as More, in connection with Bible history, greatly advanced beyond his day as he unquestionably was, and a most upright and diligent Lord Chancellor. Who could have expected the author of *Utopia* to take such a course? *Utopia*, with its admirable discussions on criminal law, its forcible objection to capital punishment for offences against property, its remarks on the tendency of the practice of inflicting needless suffering on animals, and its extraordinary latitude of toleration as to the mind! So Sir James Mackintosh summarises it. Who, then, could have imagined that the author would have become a persecutor, and an opponent of the publication of the Scriptures so that they could be understood? But *Utopia* was written when More was a young man comparatively, being thirty-eight, and far from the Lord Chancellorship of England: when the description of his household, which Erasmus gives us, is one of the loveliest pictures in literature. Here it is:—

"You would say there were in that place Plato's

* See the Facsimile Text of the first printed English New Testament, by E. Arber, 1871.

academy; but I do the house injury by comparing it to that, where there were only disputations of numbers, and geometrical figures, and moral virtues. I should rather call his house a School or University of Christian Religion, for there is none therein but readeth or studieth the liberal sciences; their special care is piety and virtue; there is no quarrelling or intemperate words heard; none seen idle; which household discipline that worthy gentleman doth not govern by proud and haughty words, but with all kind and courteous favour. Everybody performeth his duty, yet there is always alacrity; neither is sober mirth anything wanting."

But what Shakespeare says of another, may be applied both to More and his royal master:

> " For sweetest things turn sourest by their deeds;
> Lilies that fester smell far worse than weeds."

No doubt he became alarmed and indignant at some of the excesses of the Reformation party, which, however, were almost to be expected. He never thought that his *Utopia* would furnish texts for excited agitators on village greens or in the public houses of German towns, and was horrified at the Peasants' War.*

One cannot but mourn deeply over such a man, however, and see in him the natural effect of mediæval Popery. Christopher Anderson says: " *Utopia* was the blossom of his youth, but there had been little congenial moisture within him, and so it dropped off. His tedious controversial writings were the fruit of his mature age, and they remain, to any who ever look at them, the saddest memorial of his falling into the yellow leaf."

Foxe says that he was called to the works of a layman, and " if he had kept himself within his own shop, and applied the faculty whereunto he was called, and had not overreached himself to prove masteries in such matters wherein he had little skill, less experience, and which pertained not to his profession, he had deserved not only much more commendation, but also a longer life." He goes much further

* *Cambridge History of Literature.*

than this later on, and says that he was so blinded in the zeal of Popery, so deadly set against the one side, and so partially affectionate unto the other, that in them whom he favoureth he can see nothing but all fair roses and sweet virtue; in the other which he hateth, there is never a thing can please his fantasy, but all is "as black as pitch, vice, abomination, heresy, and folly, whatsoever they do, or intend to do." *

These are strong things to say, and we will justify them by giving briefly the history of Bainham, just referred to, as a sample of many more that might be given. He was a gentleman, being the son of a Gloucestershire knight, virtuously brought up, and having knowledge of Latin and Greek. He gave himself to the study of law, and became well known as a "great maintainer of the godly, a visitor of the prisoners, liberal to scholars, very merciful to his clients, using equity to the poor, very diligent in giving counsel to all the needy, widows, fatherless, and afflicted, without money or reward; briefly, a singular example to all lawyers."

Well, here was just the man that one would have expected the Lord Chancellor of England to make a friend of, and advance. The law was his profession, and the Lord Chancellor was at the head of it. But there was one thing more : " he was an earnest reader of the Scriptures," and much addicted to prayer. This was the head and front of his offending, and when he found that, in spite of his birth, learning, and goodness, it was likely to cost him his very life, for a brief season his courage gave way. But he recovered himself quickly, and stood up with the New Testament of Tyndale in his hand, exclaiming with tears, "If I should not return again to this truth, this Word of God would damn me both body and soul, at the day of judgment." He prayed to every godly man to do as he did, for he would not feel such a hell again for all the world's good. What followed ? Remember this was a gentleman of spotless character, but he said, "Christ's body is not chewed with teeth." He was the son of a

* All quotations from Foxe are from Rev. J. Pratt's edition, 8 vols.

knight, but he said that neither Sir Thomas More nor any one else could prove by Scripture that there was any Purgatory. He had a most bountiful soul, but he said that whoever preached and lived according to the Word of God had the key that bound and loosed, and the Pope had no other.

This was how he suffered. First, he lay in the Bishop of London's coalhouse in the stocks, with irons on his legs, for about a fortnight. Then he was taken to Sir Thomas More's, and there chained to a post two nights; then to Fulham, where he was cruelly handled for a week; then to the Tower, for a fortnight, where he was scourged to make him revoke his opinions; at last to Newgate, where he was visited by Latimer. When he came to the stake, he embraced it, and said—

"I am come hither, good people, accused and condemned for an heretic; Sir Thomas More being my accuser and my judge; and these be the articles that I die for, which be very truth and no heresy. I say it is lawful for every man and woman to have God's book in their mother-tongue. That the Bishop of Rome is Antichrist, and that he knoweth none other keys of heaven-gates, but only the preaching of the law and the Gospel. And that there is none other purgatory than the purgatory of Christ's blood."

Then answered one of the officers called Pave, who soon afterwards hanged himself.

"Thou liest, thou heretic! thou deniest the blessed sacrament of the altar."

"I do not deny," said Bainham, "the sacrament of Christ's body and blood as it was instituted of Christ, and used of the Apostles; but I deny your transubstantiation."

"Thou heretic!" said Pave; "set fire to him, and burn him."

When the fire had half consumed his arms and legs, he said—

"O ye papists! behold, ye look for miracles, and here now ye may see a miracle, for in this fire I feel no more

SIR T. MORE AND HIS DAUGHTER.

FROM THE PICTURE IN THE VERNON GALLERY.

7

pain than if I were in a bed of down; but it is to me as sweet as a bed of roses." *

As Maitland and others have complained of the strong language often used by the Protestants, it is only fair to say that nothing could be more utterly vulgar than some of Sir Thomas More's. We will close this unpleasant subject by giving two examples, and leaving them with our readers. To those who objected to the burning of the New Testaments he answered—

"Whoso called these books which were burned the New Testament gave them a wrong name, since they were rather Tyndale's or Luther's Testaments, it being so corrupted and changed from the good and wholesome doctrine of Christ to their own devilish heresies as to be quite another thing."

And again of Tyndale's translation of Jonah, he says—

"A book that whoso delight therein shall stand in peril that Jonas was never so swallowed up of a whale as by the delight of that book a man's soul may be so swallowed up by the devil that he shall never have the grace to get out again."

Demaus says Tyndale never defiled his pen with such Billingsgate as the remaining illustration. Tyndale had spoken disparagingly of Aquinas — too much so — and More's answer is: "This devilish drunken soul abominably blasphemes this glorious Saint of God, and calls him a falsifier of Scripture. But this drowsy drudge hath drunken so deep in the devil's dregs, that but if he wake and repent himself the sooner, he may hap to fall into the mashing fat, and turn himself into draff which the hogs of hell shall feed upon."

Tyndale was certainly severe and sometimes indelicate in handling More, as he thought that he had sold his pen in order to further his political advancement. But it may have been, partly, that Tyndale was such a thorough Reformer, and that More's mind became more conservative of old ways and thoughts as life advanced; by no means an uncommon experience. How many are hampered in

* Foxe, vol. vi.

their judgment by ancient precedent, of whom Milton exclaims, "Antiquity! Why do we stand worshipping and admiring this lifeless Colossus, that, like a carved giant, terribly menacing to children and weaklings, lifts up his club, but strikes not, and is subject to the mutiny of every sparrow?"

Certainly we will believe Sir Thomas More when he denies that he cruelly used some of the Reformers with his own hands. But, as to the binding to a tree in his garden and beating, he admits that he had caused such things to be done by the officers of the Marshalsea. And he declares that none of the so-called heretics "had wrong, but that it were for they were burned no sooner." Mr. Demaus naturally looks upon it, therefore, as very significant that on the chancel wall of old Chelsea Church, adorned with a handsome marble monument which More had in his lifetime erected for himself, there should be a memorial tablet of one of the Tyndale family. There it was placed, long afterwards, probably by some one quite ignorant of all this memorable history, and it is over it, as if in triumphant superiority.

Gairdner thinks that because similar cruelties to those suffered by Bainham were also said to be practised towards another martyr, perhaps there were neither the one nor the other. We should feel inclined to believe there were both, in view of the horrible treatment of so-called heretics again and again in this reign. But that would not hinder us from giving a place amongst the noble army of martyrs to Sir Thomas More himself. Nothing could ever be more abominable and hateful than the judicial murder of such a man, and of Fisher, the aged Bishop of Rochester. Well might Europe be stunned, and think that Henry VIII. was a fiend.

But, whatever the spirit of the age, More should not have called his opponents swine, "hell hounds that the devil hath in his kennel," and "apes that dance for the pleasure of Lucifer."

He is said to have been the first to make his mark as an orator, and in his youth he conceived the idea of

MANY A SAINT HAS BEEN IN THIS OLD FLEET PRISON.

nine pageants or emblems, representing the life of man. Death boasts that he has conquered all, but fame steps in, and says:

> "O cruel death, thy power I confound;
> When thou a noble man hast brought to ground,
> Maugre thy teeth, to live cause him shall I
> Of people in perpetual memory."

And Sir Thomas More's own fame will never fade, but whilst we think of his merry and brilliant sayings, his deep affections, his spotless honour, and his beautiful home, it is sad to think that he was also a relentless persecutor.

CHAPTER IX

Fryth

"Nothing is here for tears."

Attempts were made by Henry VIII. to capture Tyndale; overtures to induce him to return to England being unsuccessful. And when these also failed, a general consultation with the bishops and the leaders of the Universities followed. The result of which was that a Royal Proclamation was published, in May 1530, ordering all copies of the New or Old Testaments to be delivered up; and promising that, if it should appear that erroneous opinions were forsaken, the king would provide a new translation, by the joint labours of great, learned, and Catholic persons. Of this promise, Cranmer often took occasion to remind the king.

Stephen Vaughan was one of Henry VIII.'s agents abroad, and he writes to the king on May 20, 1531, "that he had shown Tyndale a clause in Cromwell's letter, saying, ' If it were possible, by good and wholesome exhortations, to convert the said Tyndale from the train and affection which he now is in, and to extirpate and take away the opinions rooted in him, I doubt not but the King's Highness would be much joyous of his conversion and amendment. And if he then would return into his realm, undoubtedly the King's Royal Majesty is so inclined to mercy, pity, and compassion, that he refuseth none which he seeth to submit themselves to the obedience and good order of the world.' In these words, I thought to be such sweetness and virtues as were able to pierce the hardest heart of the world. And, as I thought, so it came to pass. For, after sight thereof, I perceived the man to be exceeding altered, and to take the same very near unto his heart, in such wise that water stood in his eyes, and he answered, 'What gracious words are these! I assure you, if it would stand with the King's most gracious pleasure, to grant only a bare text of the Scriptures to be put forth among his people, like as is put forth among the subjects of the Emperor in these parts, and of other Christian Princes, be it of the translation of what person soever shall please His Majesty, I shall immediately make faithful promise never to write more, nor abide two days in these parts after the same, but immediately repair into his realm.'"

But the searching of the Scriptures went on, in spite of all opposition. The burning did harm to the Papal cause, as Tyndale had expected; and people were forced to believe that there must be some contrariety between the Book and the doctrines of those who handled it.

> "When they brennyd the Newe Testament,
> They pretendyd a zele very fervient,
>   To maynteyne onely Goddes honour;
> Which they sayde, with protestacyon,
> Was obscured by translacyon;
>   In Englysshe causynge moche errour.
>
> But, trueth playnly to be sayde,
> Thys was the cause why they were afrayde,
>   Least layemen shuld knowe theyr iniquiti;
> Which, through Goddes Worde is so uttered,
> As it were not possyble to be suffred,
>   Yf to rede Scripture men had lyberti."
>
> *A proper dyaloge.*

Almost as soon as Tyndale's first edition was published, there came to his help a man of a very different stamp from his earlier assistant, in the person of John Fryth.

In the valuable *Cambridge History of English Literature* recently published,* he is said to be a writer and a martyr far above most of the day in dignity and breadth, and as his history is peculiarly interesting and illustra-

---

* A. W. Ward, Litt.D., and A. R. Waller, M.A., Cambridge, 1909.

tive of the times, we must linger in his company a little.
Like George Whitfield, he was the son of an innkeeper,
and was born at Sevenoaks about 1503. He studied at
Cambridge first, and then was one of those selected by
Wolsey, on account of their talents, to be members of
his new College at Oxford. Meantime he had become
acquainted with Tyndale, and adopted many of the
teachings of the Reformation. In consequence he, with
several others, was imprisoned in a deep cellar belonging
to Wolsey's College, where the salt fish was kept. The
stench killed several of them, but Fryth was released, and
joined Tyndale abroad, helping him in his translation.
After a time he returned, and having some expectations
from the Abbot of Reading, he went there. Whatever
they were, however, he was disappointed, and was taken
up and set in the stocks as a vagrant. Here he began
speaking in Latin, and asked to see the schoolmaster of
the place, who was astonished to find a scholar there,
and soon got him released. He then went to London, but
became a marked man for his writings, and was hunted
down by Sir Thomas More, and thrown into the Tower.
Here he became acquainted with Mr. Petit, a wealthy
merchant, and member of Parliament for the City several
years. He too was imprisoned by Sir Thomas More for
assisting the Reformers in the printing of their books,
and laid in a dungeon on a pad of straw, where he
contracted a disease of which he soon afterwards died.
We simply state indisputable facts. Fryth was ordered
to be examined at Croydon, and here again comes a
remarkable piece of history probably known to few in
the pleasant and populous suburb of Brixton Hill. The
two who were taking him on foot were so impressed with
his character, knowing that the upshot of his trial was
sure to be death, that they agreed together to allow him
to escape. On each side of Brixton Hill were thick
woods, and he was to fly through those on the east into
Kent, and escape abroad. Then after a little time they
would say he had escaped on the other side, and have a
search made there. Fryth, however, absolutely refused to

fall into the plot, and said he would walk to Croydon himself if they did not take him. He believed very much as Zwingli did in the matter of the Sacrament, and that and some other things were enough for the bishops. He was martyred at Smithfield, after being for some time in Newgate. Here he was put into the dungeon under the gate, and laden with bolts and irons, his neck being made fast to a post with a collar of iron so that he could neither stand upright nor lie down. Yet in this position he continued writing, by the light of a candle, almost until his death. He was burned on the 4th of July 1533, and a priest, Dr. Coke, admonished the people that they should no more pray for him than a dog. Fryth smiled, and asked God to forgive him.

Fryth must have been of considerable assistance to Tyndale in his Bible work, but what the nature and value of that assistance was we cannot tell.

Tyndale always spoke of him with affection and gratitude, however, and in one of his letters he says:

"Brother Jacob, beloved in my heart, there lives not in whom I have so good hope and trust, and in whom my heart rejoices, as in you. Not the thousandth part so much for your learning, and what other gifts else you have, as that you will creep low by the ground, and walk in those things which the conscience may feel, and not in the imaginations of the brain; in fear, and not in boldness; in open necessary things, and not to pronounce or define of hid secrets, or things that neither help nor hinder, whether they be so or no; in unity, and not in seditious opinions; insomuch that, if you be sure you know, yet, in things that may abide leisure, you will defer, or say, till others agree with you; methinks the text requires this sense or understanding." In thus praising Fryth, Tyndale shows himself.

His writings have been published by the Religious Tract Society, and amongst them is a *Mirror, or Glass, to know Thyself*. Here he says that the prophet cried, Woe to those who coupled and knit houses together, and that woe would be verified upon many of the bishops.

"Nevertheless, this I dare say, that if a bishop who may expend four thousand marks would distribute every year but the one-half unto the poor of his diocese, giving unto one man forty shillings, and lending to another twenty nobles, to set up his occupation withal, and so give and lend as he seeth need, he should within five or six years have a flourishing diocese. And I think, verily, that his face should more be allowed before God than if he had built a thousand abbeys ; for God's commandment ought first to be done, and is much more acceptable to Him than all the works that proceed of our imaginations and foolish fantasies. He shall ask you, at the day of Judgment whether you have fed the hungry, and given drink to the thirsty, and not whether you have builded abbeys and chauntries. He shall ask you whether you have harboured the harbourless, and clothed the naked, and not whether you have gilded images, or given copes to churches. He shall ask you whether you have visited the sick, and gone to the prisoners, and not whether you have gone a pilgrimage to Walsingham or Canterbury. Therefore take good heed, and say not but that ye are warned."

Grafton calls Fryth a young man of an excellent wit and learning ; and when we read the writings of such men, we see how the Reformation had a literary and spiritual impetus quite apart from anything that Henry VIII. ever said or did.

He said to Sir Thomas More, "Grant that the Word of God, I mean the text of Scripture, may go abroad in our English tongue ; and my brother, William Tyndale, and I have done, and will promise you to write no more."

This was the spirit of both men. It was not for glosses or comments they contended, and such men never attempted to form a party, and died without forming one. There were Lutherans and Calvinists, but the term "Tyndalian" occurs only once in the letter of an enemy, and it never was adopted.

Tyndale next directed his labours to the Old Testament, learning Hebrew under the Jewish Rabbis of Germany,

in the herte, ſo that a man bringeth forth good
workes of his awne acord without compulſiõ
of the lawe, without feare of threateninges or
curſinges: yee and with out all maner reſpecte
or loue vnto any temporal pleaſure, But of the
very power of the ſprete receaved thorow faith, As thou readeſt. Ioan.i. He gaue them power to be the ſonnes of God in that they bele-
ued on his name. And of.that power they wor
ke: ſo that he which hath the ſprete of chriſt is
now no moare a childe: he nether learneth or
worketh now any longer for payne of the rodde or for feare of boogges or pleaſure of apples, But doth althinges of his awne courage
As chriſt ſayeth. Ioan.vij. He that beleueth on
me ſhall haue riuers of lyuinge water flowinge
out of his belye. That is, All good workes ãd
all giftes of grace ſpringe out of him natural-
lye and by their awne accorde. Thou neadeſt
not to wreſt good workes out of him as a mã
wold wringe veriuce out of crabbes: Nay thei
flow naturally out of him as ſpringes out off
hilles or rockes.

The newe teſtament was euer, eue from the
beginning of the world. For there were alwa-
ye promyſes of Chriſt to come by faith in whi
che promyſes the electe were then iuſtifyed
inwardly

PORTION OF TYNDALE'S PROLOGUE TO EXODUS.

*(Including the curious passage, " For payne of the rodde
or for fear of boogges.")*

and published his translation of the Pentateuch, January 17th, 1530. He gained a fair knowledge of Hebrew before attempting this work; as is evidenced by references to the subject in his works.* For instance, in his *Parable of the Wicked Mammon,* he expounds the word thus : "Mammon is a Hebrew word, and signifieth riches, or temporal goods; namely, all superfluity, and all that is above necessity, wherewith a man may help another, without undoing or hurting himself. For Hamon, in the Hebrew speech, signifieth a multitude, or plenteousness, of goods or riches." Again, speaking of St. Matthew's Hebraisms, he says: "If ought seem changed, or not altogether agreeing with the Greek, let the finder of the fault consider the Hebrew phrase, or manner of speech, left in the Greek words; whose preterperfect tense, and present tense, is oft both one; and the future tense is the optative mood also; and oft the imperative mood, in the active voice; and in the passive ever." †

Tyndale was delighted to find that this old language, new to him and to everybody, " agreed a thousand times more with the English than with the Latin"; and soon followed his translation of the Pentateuch with one of Jonah; which usually stood at the head of the Prophets in his time. There is some strong language in the Prologue. "As the envious Philistines," he says, "stopped the wells of Abraham, and filled them up with earth, to put the memorial out of mind, to the intent that they might challenge the ground; even the fleshly minded hypocrites stop up the Scripture with their traditions, false similitudes, and lying allegories, out of like zeal to make the Scripture their own possession and merchandise; and so, shut up the Kingdom of Heaven, which is God's word, neither entering in themselves, nor suffering them that would."

The Pentateuch was printed in piebald fashion; Genesis

---

* Worms had a colony of Jews, and an ancient synagogue, established, according to tradition, shortly after the destruction of the Temple by Nebuchadnezzar.

† Lewis.

A NEW LITERATURE.

and Numbers being in Gothic letter; Exodus, Leviticus, and Deuteronomy in Roman type. There is no collective title-page, and the different books were probably intended for separate issue.

Tyndale had already been hunted, and Antwerp was a dangerous place for him; but it had its advantages. Here also he translated and printed Jonah. So completely had this book disappeared, that its existence was doubted, till Lord Arthur Harvey found a copy bound up in an old volume in his library at Ickworth.

In his revision of the Pentateuch, which Tyndale also published at Antwerp, there were no changes made except in Genesis. The translation is highly idiomatic. For instance, Gen. xxxix. 2, "And the Lord was with Joseph, and he was a lucky fellow." The notes are often curious. "Enoch walked with God, and was no more seen; that is, he lived godly, and died; God took him away; that is, hid his body, as he did Moses and Aaron's, lest haply they should have made an idol of him, for he was a great preacher and a holy man." On the constantly *quœstio vexata* of faith and works, he says: "If any man ask me, seeing that faith justifieth me, why I work; I answer, Love compelleth me. For, as long as my soul feeleth what love God hath showed me in Christ, I cannot but love God again, and His will and commandments, and of love work them; nor can they seem hard unto me. I think not myself better for my working; nor seek heaven, nor a higher place in heaven, because of it." The Prologue closes: "Read God's word diligently, and with a good heart, and it shall teach thee all things."

About the same period, Luther published his German translation; Zwingli, in Switzerland, and Le Fevre, in France, also gave the Scriptures to their countrymen. And a Swedish New Testament appeared in 1521. It was indeed an age of translations. But it is not going too far to repeat that Tyndale's early translation gave the Bible which is now in common use a stamp which no subsequent editions could efface. That he did not found his work on the Vulgate, and was not greatly

8

influenced by the versions of Wycliff and Purvey, we cannot be too thankful; as also that he was not betrayed into a pedantic style, but produced a book popular and homely, whilst grave and beautiful. " A peculiar genius," says Froude, " breathes through it; in the mingled tenderness and majesty, the Saxon simplicity, the preternatural grandeur, unequalled and unapproached in the attempted improvements of modern scholars—all are here, and the impress of one man, William Tyndale."

Some portions of the Apocrypha followed. But, in 1534, an edition of his New Testament was published in Holland, edited for Christopher of Endhoven's widow by George Joye, who made considerable alterations in the text, and introduced errors based on the Old Latin version, particularly with regard to the state of the dead before the Judgment. Tyndale was naturally annoyed at this liberty. And other surreptitious reprints being made at the same time, his attention was drawn back to the New Testament. In November of the same year, therefore, he issued a new and revised edition of his own, with short marginal notes, and prologues to the several books, chiefly compiled from Luther. This was the first edition containing the name of the translator.

I am indebted to Lord Peckover for the following quaint illustrations of this edition, which is the one given in the English Hexapla:—

Matt. 14. 20.—And they gadered up of the gobbets that remayned xii baskets full.

John 1. 15.—He that cometh after me was before me, because he was yer than I.

Gal. 6. 17.—Let no man put me to busynes.

Matt. 26. 30.—When they had said grace.

Edgar gives a large number of illustrations of Tyndale's idiomatic and often forceful renderings :—

Phil. 1. 8.—I long after you all, from the very herte rote in Jesus Christ.

Mark 6. 31.—There were many comers and goers, that they had no leisure so moche as to eat.

Mark 2. 4.—They let him down thorowe the tylinge, beed and all.

2 Cor. 2. 17.—We are not as many which chopped an chaunge with the Worde of God.

Luke 22. 25.—They that bear rule over them are called gracious Lords.

1 Tim. 6. 4.—He is pufte up and knoweth nothinge, but wasteth his braynes aboute questions and stryfe of words.*

Quite a number of Tyndale's renderings that were changed in the Authorised Version have been practically restored in the Revised.

* *Bibles of England.*

CHAPTER X

"So kind an office hath been done."

THERE is no positive proof that Tyndale ever came into contact with Luther, and Mr. Anderson contends that the contrary was sent abroad by the enemies of Tyndale to damage the reputation of his work, "Lutheran" then answering to the "Lollard" of an earlier time. Mr. Offer has recently brought to light a few manuscript translations of portions of the New Testament, bearing the signature of W. T., and the date of 1502, twenty years before the publication of any portion of Luther's Bible. But both Westcott and Demaus think that these are literary forgeries, of which there have been many examples.

He lived for a time at Marburg, where he found a safer residence. The Landgrave, Philip the Magnanimous, had early and enthusiastically embraced the Reformation. On the heights above the city stood his ancient castle, and, in 1527, he had founded the University—where to-day there are a thousand students. Here the press of Hans Luft was of great service to Tyndale. He never returned to the land of his birth, for the best of reasons.

For some time he was on good terms with the English merchants at Antwerp; and several plots were laid to bring him back to England, but they failed. A beautiful description of his manner of life here is given by Foxe. He had two days in the week which he called his days of pastime, being the only ones that he did not devote to hard study. On Monday he visited such as were fled out of England on account of the persecutions, liberally

ANNE BOLEYN.
FROM THE ORIGINAL PAINTING BY HOLBEIN.

relieving them. On Saturday he walked round about the town, seeking out the poor, the aged, the weak, and those overburdened with children. These he relieved out of a liberal sum given him by the merchants at Antwerp. He was a man, says Foxe, "without any spot or blemish of rancour or malice, full of mercy and compassion, so that no man living was able to reprove him of any kind of sin."

Two attempts on Tyndale failed. We have referred to Stephen Vaughan, who was instructed to promise him safe conduct if he would return, but he had the discretion to remain where he was. Vaughan was an English envoy in the Low Countries; and then Henry issued orders for his apprehension, and sent over Sir Thomas Elyot, a friend of Sir T. More's. But Tyndale was not only in exile, but in hiding; and although Sir Thomas offered many rewards for his discovery, he had to report that, "like as he is in wit movable, so is his person uncertain to come by."

Vaughan, indeed, disapproved entirely of Sir Thomas More's crusade against the English Reformers, and admired Tyndale, though he repudiated the imputation of being a "Tyndalian" himself. Very touching was the great translator's answer to him once, when he was speaking of the king's clemency, and urging him to return to England, as we have seen.

If the Bible was translated and published at all, he would return, "and there most humbly submit myself at the feet of His Royal Majesty, offering my body to suffer what pain and torture, yea, what death his grace will, so that this be obtained. . . . But if the things I have written be true and stand with God's word, why should His Majesty, having so excellent gift of knowledge in the Scriptures, move me to do anything against my conscience?"

Fryth said practically the same when in the Tower, adding—"Till sufficient instruction is given to the poor commoners, the Word of God boileth in my body like a fervent fire, and will needs have issue, and breaketh out when occasion is given."

And let it never be misunderstood that, whilst such men died for giving the people of England the Scriptures, it was the Scriptures themselves that the Romanists raged against in vain. It was not the notes and comments, as some have ignorantly said. Every year, on the average, since the first New Testament was printed, there had been a new edition, and these were reprints of the octavo of Worms, without note or comment, except references in the margin to parallel passages. What was prohibited, condemned, and burnt was the simple text of Holy Scripture, without any note, comment, or prologue of any kind whatever.

Cochlæus never got the reward he expected for his interference at Cologne, but at least he may be credited with bidding very hard for it when he says:

"The New Testament translated into the vulgar tongue is the food of death, the fuel of sin, the vail of malice, the pretext of false liberty, the protection of disobedience, the corruption of discipline, the depravity of morals, the termination of concord, the death of honesty, the well-spring of vices, the disease of virtues, the instigation of rebellion, the milk of pride, the nourishment of contempt, the death of peace, the destruction of charity, the enemy of unity, the murderer of truth." Mr. Demaus, who quotes this from Cochlæus's *An licet Laicis,* very properly says that Romanists holding such views proscribed and burnt the Bible as naturally as people who dread contagion burn all infected garments.

Tyndale was living in the "English House," set apart, since 1474, by the municipality for the use of English merchants, when he was at length arrested. It was in a block of buildings between the present Rue de la Vieille Bourse and Rue Kirck. Tyndale had taken up his abode here in 1533, thinking himself safe from further attack. Towards the close of the year, John Rogers came as English chaplain. At first a Roman Catholic, he joined the Reformers, probably through Tyndale's influence.

Previously to this, Tyndale had turned from translation to exposition. He published an exposition of St. John's

First Epistle, and of the Sermon on the Mount. Anne Boleyn, about this time, interfered on behalf of Harman,

(THE PRESENT) BLICKLING HALL, WHERE ANNE BOLEYN WAS BORN, AND LIVED HER EARLIER LIFE. GARDENS AND LAKE.

BLICKLING HALL.

an Antwerp merchant, who had suffered losses and imprisonment for helping to circulate New Testaments. Tyndale sent to her, in gratitude, a copy of his New

Testament printed on vellum, and marked *with her name and title on the edges*,* whilst his own was suppressed. The British Museum possesses this copy.

Anne Boleyn had a double reason for being a Protestant. In the first place, her father, Sir Thomas Boleyn, was a man of learning, and a friend of Erasmus, who said that he was almost the only learned man amongst the nobility. Henry VIII. sent him on important embassies to Foreign Courts, and he thus came in contact with men of liberal views in Germany and other countries. He certainly embraced many of the new opinions, and three of the

THE LIBRARY, BLICKLING HALL.

Treatises of Erasmus were written at his request, including his exposition of the Apostles' Creed. Erasmus congratulated him on thinking more of learning than his honourable ancestry, and in one of his letters says:

" I do the more congratulate you when I observe that the sacred Scriptures are so precious to a man such as you, so powerful a layman and a courtier, and that you are actuated by a desire to possess that pearl of price."

Of course this was notorious, and Anne would be greatly

* Anna, Angliæ, Regina. When examining it in the British Museum, I found the tradition there was, that the queen took this lovely volume to the scaffold.

influenced by him in her earliest years, as well as later, when she had returned from France, so that it was perfectly natural for Shakespeare to make Wolsey say—

"What though I know her virtuous, and well-deserving? yet I know her for a spleeny Lutheran; and not wholesome to our cause. This candle burns not clear; 'tis I must snuff it."

Then again, when Anne Boleyn was a girl, and accompanied the king's sister to France, she became closely connected with Margaret of Valois, from whom she very

MARGUERITE DE VALOIS, THE QUEEN OF NAVARRE, AND HER PROTESTANT FRIENDS.

likely imbibed her Protestant views. If so, they were largely those of Erasmus, as Mr. Saintsbury tells us in his edition of the *Heptameron*. Margaret was a highly cultivated and energetic queen, and would naturally have the strongest objection to the idleness, ignorance, and often coarseness and vices of the cloister. She had aspirations after a more spiritual form of religion than the Popery of the day provided, and she sheltered many persecuted Reformers, and more than once begged for the release of some supposed heretic. There was dissension between her husband and herself in consequence, though he was at one time of her mind—never knowing his own.   The side of the Reformation which appealed to her was its spiritual pietism, and its connection with learning and letters, of which she was an ardent devotee.

Anne Boleyn was with her for some time at the most impressionable age, and often showed her Protestant feelings.   She tried to get preferment for Garrett, whose story is one of the most touching of the Reformers.   She

TYNDALE'S PRESENT TO ANNE BOLEYN

gave a copy of Fish's *Supplication of Beggars* to the king, after she and her brother had read it.   This short book is the most awful indictment of Popery in all the literature of the period, and if a quarter of it is true, the wonder is not that it fell in this reign, but that it lasted so long.   It could not fail to stir deep feelings in any one that read it, king or peasant, and Henry said, after a long pause, "If a man should pull down an old stone wall, and begin at the lower part, the upper part might chance to fall upon his head." After describing the horrible lives of many of the Friars, it exclaims:

"This is the great reason why they will not let the New Testament go abroad in your mother tongue, lest men should spy out that they do translate your kingdom into their hands; that they are cruel, unclean, unmerciful hypocrites."

Anne Boleyn was a great supporter of Protestant scholars at Cambridge, and in fact her generosity was remarkable. If any one chooses to believe the flimsily supported charges brought against her by the great bloated, cowardly wife-murderer, he may. But the average mind will find them hard to harmonise with the testimony of her silk-woman (Miss Wilkinson), who said that she kept all those about her so occupied in making shirts and smocks for the poor, that there was no idleness nor doubtful pastimes such as are commonly seen in princes' Courts. And of the Duchess of Richmond, who said that she thought no day well spent wherein some had not fared the better by some benefit at her hands. But as Wolsey once said, if the king had ordered a jury to bring in a verdict that Abel killed Cain, they would have done it. Of course she was obnoxious to the supporters of the Pope both at home and abroad, and Wyatt in his Memoirs of her ascribes her downfall to their plottings, "the most and chiefest of them having come from Rome," that

"Nest of treasons, in which is hatched and bred
What ill this day the world doth overspread,"

as Petrarch long before termed it.

Certainly Chapuys, the Imperial Ambassador, whose letters are so fully given in the *State Papers*, cannot be relied on for a moment, when he dared to speak of a Queen of England as he did. But few of her friends had any moral courage.

"When smiling fortune spreads her golden ray,
All crowd around to flatter and obey;
But when she thunders from an angry sky,
Our friends, our flatterers, and lovers fly."

CHAPTER XI

THE ETRAYAL AND MARTYRDOM OF TYNDALE

> "His blood was shed,
> In confirmation of the noblest claim,
> Our claim to feed upon immortal truth,
> To walk with God, to be divinely free,
> To soar, and to anticipate the skies.
>
> O pitiless skies! why did your clouds retain,
> For peasants' fields their floods of hoarded rain!
> O pitiless earth! why opened no abyss,
> To bury in its chasm a crime like this!"

In 1535 Tyndale made the acquaintance of the miscreant, Phillips, who betrayed him. He was said to have been a Roman Catholic student at Louvain, but had fled to Flanders, after robbing his father. He insinuated himself into Tyndale's confidence, by professing great zeal for religious reform. Then he borrowed some money from him, decoyed him from the "English House," and betrayed him to the Imperial officers on 23rd May 1535. Mr. Carlyle says that it cannot be proved that this wretch was either the agent of Henry VIII., or a tool of English Catholics. But he must have been somebody's tool; and, no doubt, he was well paid for his Judas-work.*

Cromwell dispatched a Cambridge scholar to Louvain to find out how Phillips was supplied with funds, and doubtless to stop the supplies, if possible; a very practical measure. It was thus discovered that Phillips had two benefices and a prebend when he went over the sea, and his employers would be sure to transmit the traitorous pluralist his revenues. "It was therefore the funds of

---

* E. Irving Carlyle, in *Biographical Dictionary*.

the Church of England," says Demaus, Tyndale's biographer, "those funds which the piety of previous
generations had consecrated for the perpetual religious
benefit of the community, which were employed in doing
to death the man who has bestowed upon the people of
England the greatest religious blessing which they enjoy."

In fact, Mr. Carlyle has not made himself quite familiar
enough with his edition of Foxe. There he would have
read (vol. v. p. 121) :—

"In the Registers of London it appeareth manifest how

THE ENGLISH HOUSE, ANTWERP.

that the Bishops and Sir Thomas More having any poor
man under *coram*, to be examined before them, namely,
such as had been at Antwerp, most studiously would
search and examine all things belonging to Tyndale,
where and with whom he hosted, whereabouts stood
the house, what was his stature, in what apparel he
went, what resort he had, etc.; all which things when
they had diligently learned (as may appear by the
examination of Simon Smith and others), then began
they to work their feats."

And let not Foxe's statements be doubted. His *Acts*

and Monuments are worth far more than all the histories put together, and no man was more careful of his facts, though in eight great volumes a few inaccuracies may be found. One such, with regard to John Marbeck of Windsor, he publicly corrected, showing how he had been misled by the records and registers, the bishop's certificate and the writ of execution, into thinking that he suffered with some others. He just escaped, however.

TYNDALE'S BETRAYAL.

Persons, Harpsfield, and other contemporary Romanists, who had every means, as well as disposition, to impeach Foxe's statements, could only find two supposed errors in all the mass of his writings on the Marian persecutions. One of these was only an error of a name, and the other, after personal inquiry on the spot, was found to be no error at all.*

* *Church History of England,* J. A. Baxter, M.A.

So that Rev. Canon Townsend may well say that there is no historian of his own times so faithful, and that but for his mighty work the heart of England would never have been so permanently animated with that utter abhorrence of persecution which has been the foundation both of our liberty and our national influence amongst mankind. " In this sense John Foxe deserves to be placed, where our fathers ranked him, amongst the best friends and benefactors of the civilised world."

As it has been the fashion with some to disparage Foxe, we will add one more testimony, that of Wordsworth in his *Ecclesiastical Biography* :

"It never will be proved that John Foxe is not one of the most faithful and authentic of all historians. We know too much of the strength of Foxe's book, and the weakness of those of his adversaries. The many researches and discoveries of later times, in regard to historical documents, have only contributed to place the general fidelity and truth of Foxe's melancholy narrative on a rock which cannot be shaken." And this in spite of the fact that Foxe's great work is twice as long as Gibbon's *Decline and Fall,* and is perhaps without a parallel in literature. My edition contains 6700 pages, largest octavo, being Rev. J. Pratt's. "Homely, dramatic, and vital," says the *Cambridge History of Literature.*

Tyndale was thrown into prison at Vilvorde, near Brussels ; where he remained about a year and a half. Before this, however, he prepared a further edition of the New Testament, without any marginal notes, which has been supposed to have a rustic orthography, and to redeem his promise of giving God's word to the Gloucestershire ploughboys. But this idea is without foundation ; the probability being that some Flemish compositor, who issued the work after Tyndale's arrest, and without his supervision, introduced Flemish equivalents for the English vowel sounds.

Another still more absurd idea is that Tyndale was in this volume attempting phonological reform, bringing spelling and pronunciation into correspondence.

9

Two editions, in fact, appeared in 1535; the first, from the press of Hans van Ruremonde, at Antwerp, being an octavo. This is the one thought to be for Gloucestershire ploughboys.* Probably it was a private enterprise of Dutch printers, who wished to anticipate the final revision which Tyndale was understood to be preparing. This last revision has the signature G.H.; and Mr. Bradshaw has now shown that this stands for Godfried van der Haghen, the Antwerp publisher, who possibly employed Martin Emperour as his printer. It was a dangerous thing to avow sympathy with a man like Tyndale, so there is no printer's name; and the publisher simply inserted his initials.

Here is a sample of the 1535 Testament, with the peculiar spelling. " Though I spaeke with the tonges of men and aengels, and yet had no love, I were even as soundynge brasse, or as a tinklinge cimball. And though I could prophesy, and ondestoede all secretes, and all knowledge ; ye, yf I had all faeyth, so that I coulde move mountayns oute of thear places, and yet had no love, I were nothinge." It was simply the Flemish printers who put in their own spelling.

Foxe says that, during his imprisonment, Tyndale converted his keeper, the keeper's daughter, and others of his household. The rest that knew him said that, if he were not a good Christian man, they could not tell who to trust. Probably Tyndale left behind him a translation of Joshua, Judges, Ruth, Samuel, Kings, and Chronicles, completed while in " durance vile."

It was a real prison, however. And from a letter still extant, written to the Governor, we gain a sorrowful insight into his prison life Tyndale pathetically appeals for " a warmer cap, for I suffer extremely from cold in the head, being afflicted with a perpetual catarrh, which is considerably increased in the cell ; also a piece of cloth, to patch my leggings. My overcoat has been worn out. My

* The Cambridge University Library has a copy. Father is spelled " faether " ; master, " maester " ; stone, " stoene " ; once, " oones " ; worse, " whorsse."

shirts are also worn out. I wish also his permission to
have a candle in the evening; for it is wearisome to sit
alone in the dark."

This is the only letter of Tyndale's extant. It reminds
us of the pathetic close of St. Paul's Second Epistle to
Timothy. Not a single letter, or document of any sort,
in his own hand, had been discovered, till this was found

THE CASTLE OF VILVORDE, NEAR BRUSSELS.
FROM THE "LIFE OF TYNDALE," BY R. DEMAUS, M.A.

by a foreigner. M. Galesloot came across it in the archives
of the Council of Brabant. Mr. F. Fry had it photographed;
and the facsimile is amongst the treasures in the large
room of the British Museum Library. The letter has
neither date nor superscription. But there is not the
least doubt that it was written at Vilvorde, in the winter
of 1535, and addressed to the Governor of the Castle, the

Marquis Bergen op Zoom, with whom Cromwell had lately interceded in Tyndale's favour. He had been appointed Governor in 1530. A huge whitewashed Penitentiary occupies the site of the old castle now, having been built in 1870. The larger castle in which Tyndale was imprisoned was built by Duke Wenceslaus in 1375, and the archives of Brabant were kept there, in addition to State prisoners.

A discussion, conducted in a better spirit than most such, took place between Tyndale and some Louvain theologians; but it could only end in one way. After the mouse is played with, it is devoured.

Some earnest efforts, however, were made to save Tyndale's life, especially by his faithful Antwerp friend, Poyntz. And the Vaughan before alluded to wrote to Cromwell : " If now you send me your letter to the Privy Council, I could deliver Tyndale from the fire ; so it come by time." Henry VIII. was on bad terms with the Emperor Charles V., however, and it was the Emperor that ordered the execution. So that, for this foul murder, at all events, England is not responsible. Indeed, in England, the great subject of all this time was the king's divorce ; and the appearance of the Bible in an English dress was quite a secondary matter. Cranmer did nothing to save Tyndale, though he knew all ; but probably there was nothing he could do. Thus, on the 6th October 1536, Tyndale was led forth to the stake ; and, after being strangled, his body was consumed to ashes.

He died praying, " Lord, open the King of England's eyes," with a fervent zeal and a loud voice, and his prayer was answered at once. Before the waning year had come to its close, the first volume of Scripture ever printed on English ground came forth from the press of the king's own printer ; and that volume was a folio Testament, Tyndale's own version, with his prologues too, and with the long proscribed name of William Tyndale openly set forth on its title-page.* The next

* Probably printed by Thomas Berthelet, though his name is not mentioned, and at the very time when Tyndale was being martyred.

MARTYRDOM OF TYNDALE.

year, the whole Bible, including a large portion translated by Tyndale, was sanctioned by the king, for was there not found in it, "The king's heart is in the hands of the Lord; as the rivers of water He turneth it whithersoever He will." *

We are indebted to the valuable *Life of Tyndale*, by the Rev. R. Demaus, M.A., for a view of the Castle of Vilvorde, where the martyr was imprisoned, strangled, and burned to death. The traveller who is approaching Brussels looks in vain for any sign of its existence, for not one stone has been left upon another. But Vilvorde has two church towers, and is now a pleasant enough place, as I saw it a few summers ago, when the peasants were hay-making.

Memorials have been raised to Tyndale's memory, both in Gloucestershire and in London, where he began his work. A monument, in the form of a fine column, 122 feet in height, and 26 feet square at the base, has recently been erected by subscription, on a site at North Nibley Knoll, Gloucestershire, given by Earl Fitzhardinge. This was then supposed to be his birthplace. The monument was unveiled by the Earl of Ducie, 6th November 1866. The project for this memorial was originally made by Mr. C. Anderson, whose admirable work on the English Bible is so largely a life of Tyndale. It was revived in 1861 by a few gentlemen living near Nibley.

Another memorial graces the Thames Embankment, being a bronze statue by Mr. J. E. Boehm, costing about £2400. Mr. Tyssen Amherst, afterwards Lord Amherst of Didlington Hall, Norfolk, obtained a fine site from the Metropolitan Board of Works; and Dean Stanley, in presiding at the first public meeting to promote it, said that the work of revision, then in progress, "was but the latest edition of Tyndale's Bible." The statue

---

Christopher Anderson thinks that Anne Boleyn must have patronised it, or it could scarcely have been issued from the king's printers. This would harmonise with her defence of Harman.

* Life, in Parker Society's *Doctrinal Treatises*.

was unveiled by the Earl of Shaftesbury, 7th May 1884. It is ten feet in height, and one-half the money was guaranteed by twelve gentlemen.

So Tyndale has not been neglected, by our generation at least, though the lines are often true :

> "Patriots have toiled ; and, in their country's cause,
> Bled nobly. And their deeds, as they deserve,
> Receive proud recompense. We give in charge
> Their names to the sweet lyre. The historic muse,
> Vain of the treasure, marches with it down
> To latest times. And Scripture, in her turn,
> Gives bond in stone, and ever-during brass,
> To guard them, and to immortalise her trust.
> But fairer wreaths are due, though never paid
> To those who, posted at the shrine of truth,
> Have fallen in her defence."

It was openly acknowledged in the Convocation of 1536, by Fox, Bishop of Hereford, before Tyndale expired, that " the lay people do now know the Scriptures better than many of us." And, though Henry VIII.'s sanction of the Bible was only " the whim of a moment," the people, lay and clerical, of England have been doing perpetual honour to Tyndale's memory by using what is so largely his work. But Tyndale never sought human praise, for, as he said in one of his prologues, " He that hath the Spirit of Christ, neither learneth, nor worketh, for payne of the rodde, or for feare of boogies, or pleasure of apples."

Erasmus died during the same year. And Tyndale's convert and coadjutor, John Rogers, was the first martyr in the bloody days of Queen Mary. Truly, in these, as in many times before, the blood of the martyrs was the seed of the Church ; and we see how that seed has brought forth in us a hundredfold, in a long harvest of peaceful days. To lead the way is always harder than to follow. Thus to Tyndale belongs the double praise, of having stamped the English Bible with his own high character, and braved the dangers incident to such a work.

Of the five or six editions of Tyndale's first New Testament, it is now difficult to find even a fragment. They were intercepted, captiously examined, and studiously misrepresented. "There is not so much as one i therein, if it lacke a tytle over his hed, but they have noted it, and number it unto the ignorant people for an heresy." So Tyndale wrote in his Preface to the Pentateuch, published in 1530.

CHAPTER XII

TYNDALE'S OTHER WORKS

"Its wearing fatigues, its small enmities, its false friendships, and its
meagre and capricious rewards."

LYTTON on Literature.

"THE most interesting book in the language," as it has
been called, is at the Baptist College, Bristol. This is the
octavo printed at Worms, by Schoeffer, the first English
New Testament ever printed. It was originally in the
Harleian Collection, and was obtained for the Earl of
Oxford, by one of the many agents whom he employed in
hunting up such treasures. The Earl was so pleased,
when he found himself the possessor of this volume, that
he settled an annuity of twenty pounds upon the finder.
It is stated, that Osborn, the bookseller, purchased the
Harleian Library for less than the Earl had spent on the
bindings; and that, to ensure a speedy sale, he catalogued
the books at a very low figure. Not recognising the value
of this one, he priced it at fifteen shillings. It passed into
the hands of the antiquary, J. Ames; and at his death,
into those of a Mr. White, who gave fourteen guineas for
it. Mr. White sold it to his friend, Dr. Gifford, a Baptist
minister, of much repute in his day, for twenty guineas.
And Dr. Gifford placed it in the College Library. It has
been admirably reproduced in facsimile by Mr. F. Fry.

"The noble army of martyrs praise Thee." Tyndale
was one of the noblest of them; and, for a long time, he
expected no other fate. Once he said, "There is none
other way into the kingdom of life, than through persecution, and suffering, and pain, and of very death, after
the example of Christ." On another occasion he said, "If

they shall burn me, they shall do none other thing than I looked for."

But let it not be thought that he died as a disloyal and law-breaking fanatic. He said, indeed, in his *Parable of the Wicked Mammon* (1528), that there is no right of absolute ownership, apart from social obligations. And this led Sir Thomas More to call it "a very treasury and well-spring of wickedne:s." But Tyndale was quite correct; and, in the *Obedience of a Christian Man*" (1528), he defends the Reformers against the charge of disobedience to the civil power. In this, for the first time, are clearly stated the two great principles of the Reformation; namely, the supreme authority of Scripture in the Church, and of the king in the State. The treatise was shown to Henry VIII., who approved. But Tyndale's *Practice of Prelates* attacked both Henry's divorce proceedings, and Wolsey's action. This quite destroyed, in Henry's mind, the favourable impression made by the *Obedience*, as we have seen. In later editions, the part about the divorce was expunged.

In this *Obedience of a Christian Man*, Tyndale attacks, of course, the false obedience preached up in his time. "If thou pollest thy head in the worship of thy father, and breakest his commandments, shouldest thou so escape? Or, if thou painted thy master's image on a wall, and stickest up a candle before it, shouldest thou therewith make satisfaction for the breaking of his commandments? Or, if thou wearest a blue coat in the worship of the king, and breakest his laws, shouldest thou so go quiet?"

In fact, Tyndale was quite as much one of the leading writers of his age as a translator, and to those of his day the probability is that he loomed largest as a theological pamphleteer.

In the Preface he amplifies his charge of the ignorance of the clergy. After his conversations with them in Gloucestershire, he had said he would make the ploughboys understand the Scriptures better than they did, and here he says:

"Alas, the curates themselves, for the most part, wot no more what the New or Old Testament meaneth than do the Turks; neither care they, but even to mumble up so much every day, as the pie and popinjay speak. If they will not let the layman have the Word of God in his mother tongue, yet let the priests have it; which for a great part of them do understand no Latin at all, but sing, and say, and patter all day, with the lips only, that which the heart understandeth not. Christ commanded to search the Scriptures. Though miracles bare record unto His doctrine, yet desired He no faith to be given to it or to His miracles without record of the Scripture."

Under the influence of Barnes, Tyndale cast off transubstantiation, and went back to the ancient way of understanding the Sacrament; and as a final sample of the venom of Sir Thomas More, this is the way he speaks of Tyndale's giving up the gross error of his education: "But within a while after, as he that is falling is soon put over, the Friar (Barnes) made the fool mad outright, and brought him down blindfold into the deepest dungeon of that devilish heresy wherein he sitteth now, fast bounden in the chair of pestilence with the chain of pertinacity." "Our Saviour will say to Tyndale, 'Thou art accursed, Tyndale, the son of the devil, for neither flesh nor blood hath taught thee these heresies, but thine own father, the devil. Ah! blasphemous beast, to whose roaring and lowing no good Christian can without heaviness of heart give ear.'"

This from a literary man! And Maitland thinks the language of the Protestants was too strong!

It certainly seems as if Tyndale should have escaped martyrdom. Sir T. More had fallen, although only the year before, and Bishop Fisher, with his new cardinal's hat. Cranmer and Cromwell were strongly in sympathy with the Reformers. Also Miles Coverdale, his former associate, was then engaged upon the translation of the whole Scripture. Moreover, there is no doubt that Cromwell tried to save him; his imprisonment lasting sixteen months.

A fine heroic figure Tyndale presents, however, and we have had great pleasure in dwelling at some length on the notable work he did for England and for Englishmen. Sir Philip Sydney has said that the historian is " laden

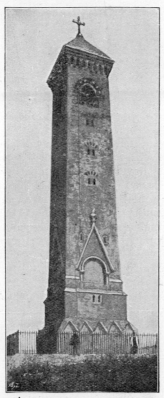

TYNDALE'S MONUMENT. AT HIS BIRTHPLACE,
EITHER NORTH NIBLEY, OR NEAR IT.

with old mouse-eaten records, authorising himself, for the most part, upon other histories, whose greatest authorities are built upon the notable foundation Hearsay; having much ado to accord differing writers, and to pick truth

out of partiality." It is not a very flattering description.
But we will set over against it Colton's dictum that, to
cite the examples of history, in order to animate men to
virtue, or to arm them to fortitude,—this is to call up
the illustrious dead to inspire and improve the living.
And of Tyndale, it may certainly be said—

> " He neither feared the darkest hour,
>   Nor trembled at the tempter's power."

T. Russell, M.A., published a portion of Tyndale's Works,
and Fryth's, in 1827.* He intended to complete his work;
but the abridged series published by the Religious Tract
Society made it impossible. The publisher complains that
there is not room for them both, and that this is not the
first time that the R.T.S., a great Society, with practically
unlimited means, has competed with the private publisher.
One cannot but have a little sympathy with the com-
plainant, but these three large volumes are a valuable
contribution to the Tyndale literature. The Prefaces are
all given; and, in that to the Pentateuch, the language
is certainly strong. " In this they be all agreed: to drive
you from the knowledge of the Scripture, and that you
shall not have the text thereof in the mother tongue;
and to keep the world still in darkness, to the intent they
might sit in the consciences of the people, through vain
superstition, and false doctrine; to satisfy their filthy
lusts, their proud ambition, and their unsatiable covetousness. . . . A thousand books had they leaver to be put
forth, against their abominable doings and doctrine, than
that the Scripture should come to light."

Tyndale shows his knowledge of Hebrew in this Preface; and says that, when he had translated the New
Testament, he desired, in an epistle at the end, any that
were learned to amend anything that was amiss. " But our
malicious and wily hypocrites, which are so stubborn and
hard-hearted in their wicked abominations, that it is not
possible for them to amend anything at all, say, some of
them, that it is impossible to translate the Scriptures

* E. Palmer, London.

into English; some, that it is not lawful for the lay-people to have it in their mother tongue; some, that it would make them all heretics. As it would, no doubt, from many things which they of long time have falsely taught. And that is the whole cause wherefore they forbid it; though they other cloaks present."

In another Prologue, to the Books of Moses, speaking of a man having a precious jewel, and yet being none the richer, because he is ignorant of its worth, Tyndale says: " It is not enough, therefore, to read and talk of it only, but we must also desire God, day and night, instantly to open our eyes, and to make us understand and feel wherefore the Scripture was given, that we may apply the medicine of the Scripture, every man to his own sores. Unless we intend to be idle disputers, and brawlers about vain words, ever gnawing upon the bitter bark without, and never attaining unto the sweet pith within; and persecuting one another in defending of lewd imaginations and phantasies of our own invention."

Tyndale wants to make all plain to the unlettered reader. And there are Tables expounding words of importance. Take a few extracts from the Table on Genesis:—

" *Bless.*—God's blessings are His gifts: as in the first chapter, He blessed them, saying, ' Grow, and multiply, and have dominion.' And in the ninth chapter, ' He blessed Noah and his sons, and gave them dominion over all beasts, and authority to eat them.' "

" *Curse.*—God's curse is the taking away of His benefits; as God cursed the earth, and made it barren. So now, hunger, dearth, war, pestilence, and such like are yet right curses, and signs of the wrath of God unto the un-believers; but, unto them that know Christ, they are very blessings, and that wholesome cross, and true pur-gatory of our flesh, through which all must go that will live godly and be saved. As thou readest in Matthew v., ' Blessed are they that suffer persecution for righteous-ness sake.' "

" *Faith* is the believing of God's promises, and a sure

trust in the goodness and truth of God. Good works are things of God's commandment, wrought in faith. And to sew a shoe at the commandment of God, to do thy neighbour service withal, with faith to be saved by Christ, is much better than to build an abbey of thine own imagination, trusting to be saved by the feigned works of hypocrites."

The Prologues are all able productions. In that to Exodus, he says :—

" Beware of subtle allegories. And note everything earnestly, as things pertaining to thine own heart and soul. . . . Note, how God is found true at the last; and how, when all is past remedy, and brought into desperation, He then fulfilleth His promises; and that by an abject and a castaway, a despised and a refused person ; yea, and by a way impossible to believe."

" Make not Moses a figure of Christ, with Rochester; but an example unto all princes, and to all that are in authority, how to rule unto God's good pleasure, and unto their neighbours' profit. For there is not a perfecter life in this world, both to the honour of God and profit of his neighbour, nor yet a greater cross, than to rule Christianly.

" Note also, how God sendeth His promise to the people, and Moses confirmeth it with miracles, and the people believe. But, when temptation cometh, they fall into unbelief, and few bide standing, where thou seest that all be not Christian that will be so called, and that the cross trieth the true and the feigned; for, if the cross were not, Christ should have disciples enough. Whereof also thou seest, what an excellent gift true faith is, and impossible to be had without the Spirit of God. For it is above all natural power that a man, in time of temptation, when God scourgeth him, should believe then steadfastly how God loveth him, and careth for him, and hath prepared all good things for him."

Beautifully Tyndale dwells on the humanity and kindliness of the law, and the reasonableness of every precept. And, as to the multitude of sacrifices and ceremonies, they were to occupy the minds of the people, and that they should have no desire to follow the heathen. But " he that goeth about to purchase grace with ceremonies doth but suck the ale-pole to quench his thirst."

Tyndale's Introduction to Leviticus shows more fully the scope of the sacrifices. He says that, though all the sacrifices and ceremonies have a starlight of Christ, yet some have the light of the broad day, and express Him as plainly as if we should play His passion on a scaffold, or in a stage play : as the scapegoat, the brazen serpent, the ox burned without the host, the passover lamb, etc. " Insomuch that I am fully persuaded that God showed Moses the secrets of Christ, and the very manner of His death."

Concerning Numbers, Tyndale says we have here the practice of the Law given by God. But then, just as in modern times, good deeds of men's own imagination were put in the place of it. The Papists " have set up wilful poverty, of another manner than any that is commanded of God. And, the chastity of matrimony utterly defied, they have set up another wilful chastity, not required of God ; which they swear, vow, and profess to give to God, whether He will give it them or no ; and compel all their disciples thereunto, saying that it is in the power of every man's free-will to observe it, contrary to Christ and His apostle Paul. And into what corrupting of other men's wives, and open whoredom, and into other abominations too filthy to be spoken of, hath their voluntary chastity brought them."

Of Deuteronomy, Tyndale says that it is worthy to be read day and night, and never to be out of our hands. The notes and glosses are nearly all his own, and not Luther's.

There follow, in these three handsome and beautifully printed volumes, *The Prologue to Jonah*, *The Wicked Mammon*, *The Obedience of a Christian Man*, *The Practice of Prelates*, *The Answer to More*, *The Prologues to the Sermon on the Mount* and *1st Epistle of John*, and *The Pathway into the Holy Scripture*.

In all that he thus wrote, Tyndale was actuated by the highest motives. " I take God to record," he cries, " if I

10

wrote of all . . . save only of pity on the blindness of my
brethren; to make every one of them, if it were possible,
as perfect as an angel of heaven." But whatever bore
his name was soon forbidden. And when the sacred
text could no longer be prohibited, all Prologues and
Annotations, by whomsoever written, were ordered to be
utterly removed from it. This is the reason why, among
the earlier editions which have come down to us, the
greater part are mutilated and defaced. Edition followed
edition, however, and the light could not be hid.

Those who want full particulars of the great number
printed must refer to the valuable work of Dr. Cotton.
He published a second edition of his list, thirty-one years
after the first, in which he mourns that, after being
within easy reach of the great libraries in London,
Oxford, and Cambridge, he had now for a long time been
in a country place in the South of Ireland. He was then
Archdeacon of Cashel; but he continued his investigations to the last. The catalogue of Mr. Lea Wilson's
library is also very valuable.

In the British Museum there are eleven German
editions of the Bible, from 1466–1518, three Bohemian,
one Dutch, 1477; five French, 1510–1531; and seven
Italian, 1471–1532. In Germany there were, in this
early age, seventy-two partial translations, and fifty
complete. Luther, in making his, had one of these
translations before him. In France these translations
were *livres de luxe*.

Certainly we were far behind in England; Caxton not
daring to print the Bible as such, on account of Arundel's
decree. But the place was partly supplied by his
Golden Legend, which came out before the close of the
fifteenth century. This contained nearly all the Pentateuch,
and the Gospel narrative, in English.

It was a folio volume, and contained the word " breches,"
in Gen. iii. 21, long before the Genevan Bible. There
were numerous editions of this book; and it was possibly
read in the Churches. The text is mixed with much
priestly gloss and dross; but the Pentateuch and the

Gospels would give anything value, and it must have been extensively read, long before the Reformation.

Mr. Francis Fry published the Tyndale in the Baptist College, Bristol, 1862. Mr. Arber reprinted the quarto fragment of the first edition. Those who wish to see the sequence of the different editions of Tyndale's Testament will find it in Mr. Fry's Bibliographical Description, printed in 1878, and full of interest.

Fuller draws a parallel between St. Paul and Tyndale. After saying that Bale called Tyndale the Apostle of the English, he says that St. Paul defeated the power of Elymas, the sorcerer, and Tyndale put a magician out of countenance. St. Paul, in Philippi, converted his jailer and his household; Tyndale, during his imprisonment at Vilvorde converted his keeper, his daughter, and others of his family. St. Paul was in perils by waters, by robbers, and amongst false brethren; and so was Tyndale.

But no man could speak out against the gross scandals of the time, and expect to escape persecution. The beautiful religion of Christ had become identified with a senseless mummery which neither appealed to the heart nor the intellect, and greed and extortion were the commonest things. "The parson sheareth, the vicar shaveth, the parish priest polleth, the friar scrapeth, and the pardoner pareth; we lack but a butcher to pull off the skin." * So Tyndale said, and this witness was true.

SPECIMENS

OF

TYNDALE'S VERSIONS

OF DIFFERENT PARTS OF THE HOLY SCRIPTURES

I. A specimen of his earliest production as a translator of Hebrew; copied from the second edition of his version of Genesis, as printed at Marburg in Hesse, by Hans Luft, and carried through the press in 1534.

---

* *Bibles of England*, Edgar.

Genesis iv. 3

AND it fortuned in processe of tyme, that Cain brought of the frute of the erth, an offeringe vnto the lorde. And Abel, he brought also of the firstlynges of his shepe ād of the fat of them. And the lorde loked vnto Abel and to his offeringe : but vnto Cain and vnto his offeringe, loked he not. And Cain was wroth exceadingly, and loured. And the lorde sayde vnto Cain : why arte thou angry, and why loureste thou ? wotest thou not yf thou do well thou shalt receave it ? But and yf thou do euell, by and by thy sinne lyeth open in the dore : notwithstondinge let it be subdued unto the, and se thou rule it. And Cain talked with Abel his brother.

And assoone as they were in the feldes Cain fell vpon Abel his brother and slewe him. And the Lorde sayd vnto Cain : where is Abel thy brother ? And he sayd : I can not tell, am I my brothers keper ? And he sayde : What haste thou done ? the voyce of thy brothers bloud cryeth vnto me out of the erth. And now cursed be thou as pertayninge to the erth, whiche openned her mouth to receaue thy brothers bloud of thine hande. For when thou tyllest the grounde she shall henceforth not geue hyr power vnto the. A vagabunde and a rennagate shall thou be vpon the erth.

And Cain sayd vnto the lorde : my sinne is greater, then that it maye be forgeuen. Beholde thou castest me out this daye frō of the face of the erth, and frome thy syght must I hyde my selfe, and I must be wandringe and a vagabunde vpon the erth. Morouer whosoeuer findeth me, will kill me. And the lorde sayd vnto him. Not so, but whosoeuer slayeth Cain, shalbe punysshed vii. folde. And the Lorde put a marke vpon Cain that no man that founde hym, shulde kyll him. And Cain went out from the face of the Lorde and dwelt in the lande Nod, on the east syde of Eden.

II. A specimen of Tyndale's latest labours as a translator of Hebrew ; copied from his version of the historical books of the Old Testament, as incorporated by Rogers into the Bible called Matthew's, and first published by Grafton the printer in 1537, about ten months after the translator's martyrdom.

2 SAMUEL i. 17

And Dauid sang thys song of mournyng ouer Saul and ouer Jonathas hys sonne, & bad to teache the children of Israel ye staues therof. And Beholde it is wryttē in the boke of ryghtwes. The glorye of Israell is slayne upō ye hie hilles: Oh how were ye mightye ouerthrowē? Tell it not in Geth: nor publyshe it in the streates of Askalon: lest the daughters of the Philistines rejoise, & that ye daughters of ye uncircūcised triūphe therof. Ye mountaynes of Gelboe, upon you be nether dew nor raygne, ner feldes whence heaue offeringes come. For there the shildes of ye myghtie were cast from them: the shilde of Saul, as though he had not bene anoynted wyth oyle. The boowe of Jonathas and the swerde of Saul turned neuer backe agayne emptie, from the bloud of the wounded and from the fatte of the mightie warryowres.

Saul and Jonathas louely and pleasaūt in their lyues, were in their deethes not deuided, men swiftter then Egles and stronger then Lyons. Ye daughters of Israel, wepe ouer Saul, whych clothed you in purple & garmentes of pleasure, and bordered youre rayment with ornamentes of goulde. How were ye mightye slayne in battell? Jonathas on the hie hilles was wounded to deeth. Woo is me for the my brother Jonathas: delectable to me wast thou excedyng. Thy loue to me was wonderfull, passing ye loue of wemē. How were thy myghtie ouerthrowen, & how were the wepons of warre forloren.

III. A specimen of Tyndale's labours as a translator of Greek; from the earliest edition of his version of the new Testament printed at Worms, in 1525, and now in the library of the Baptist College, Bristol.

1 CORINTHIANS xiii.

Though I speake with the tongs of men ād angels, and yet had no love, I were evē as soundynge brasse: and as

a tynklynge Cynball. and though I coulde prophesy, and
vnderstode all secretes, and all knowledge : yee, if I had
all fayth so that I coulde move mountayns oute of there
plac^s, and yet had no love, I were nothynge.   And though
I bestowed all my gooddès to fede the povre, and though
I gave my body even that I burned, ād yet have no love,
it profeteth me nothynge.

Love suffreth lōge, and is corteous.   love envieth nott.
Love doth nott frawardly, swelleth not, dealeth not dis-
honestly, seketh nott her awne, is not provoked to anger,
thynketh not evyll, reioyseth not in iniquite : but reioyseth
in the trueth, suffreth all thynge, beleveth all thyng^s
hopeth all thyng^s, endureth ī all thyng^s.   Though that
prophesyinge fayle, other tonges shall cease, or knowledge
vanysshe awaye : yet love falleth never awaye.

For oure knowledge is vnparfet, and oure prophesyīge
is vnperfet : but whē thatt which is parfet is come : thē
that which is vnparfet shall bedone awaye.   When I was
a chylde, I spake as a chylde, I vnderstode as a childe, I
ymmagened as a chylde : but as sone as I was a man I
put awaye all childesshnes.   Nowe we se in a glasse even
in a darke speakynge : but then shall we se face to face.
Nowe I knowe vnparfectly : but then shall I knowe even
as I am knowen.   Nowe abideth fayth, hope, and love,
even these thre : but the chefe of these is love.

CHAPTER XIII

THE FIRST COMPLETE ENGLISH BIBLE—COVERDALE

"There is a fragrance which can never waste,
Though left for ages to the charter'd wind."

BUT " the immortals never come alone," and we must look in another direction to find the first entire Bible printed in the English tongue. To Miles Coverdale, a Cambridge scholar, this work has been universally ascribed ; and he probably hailed from the same part of Yorkshire as Wycliff had done before him. He had acquaintances amongst the highest in the land, being a visitor at the house of Sir T. More. His early patron was Cromwell, the favourite of Henry VIII. through a long period ; and his connection with him frequently saved him from trouble.

Coverdale early imbibed the principles of the Reformation ; and, whilst at the University, became a diligent student of the Scriptures. He was, for a considerable time, in the Monastery of the Augustine's at Cambridge, of which the well-known Dr. Barnes was Prior ; and they appear to have thrown off the errors of Popery together. The meetings of those who inclined to Protestantism were held frequently at a house called the " White Horse," which came, from this association, to be nick-named " Germany," the Reformed doctrines being imported thence. They could easily meet here from the principal Colleges.

This was in 1526, just after the publication of Tyndale's first New Testament ; and partly, no doubt, in consequence of it. When Barnes was arrested, and conveyed to London, Coverdale attended him, and helped him to prepare his defence, laying aside his conventual habit. Later on, we find him preaching at Binstead, in Essex, against transubstantiation and the worship of images, and conversing privately with a priest against confession, so that his safety became endangered. Hollinshed thus portrays his character: "He was very sober in diet, godlie in life, friendlie to the godlie, liberal to the poor, and courteous to all men, void of pride, full of humilitie, abhorring covetousness, and an enemy to all wickedness and wicked men."

It is not known how long Coverdale was engaged in his Bible work. But we lose sight of him from 1528 to 1535; and probably he left England. It is likely that Zurich was the scene of his labours; and that he visited and spent some time with Tyndale, at Hamburg. Probably both Cromwell and Sir T. More had to do with Coverdale's undertaking the translation of the Scriptures. In a letter addressed to the former, he speaks of beginning to taste of Holy Scripture, and of being "set to the most sweet smell of holy letters." Certainly it was sweet work to him, and there is much tender beauty about many of his renderings.

Yes, Zurich, the city of Zwingli, who, fourteen years before, had opposed Samson in his impious traffic of Indulgences, just as Luther had opposed Tetzel. At least, in the main, Coverdale's version is based on the Swiss-German Version produced by Zwingli; and Leo Juda, which was published at Zurich; also on the Latin of Pagninus.*

About ten years after the New Testament, on 4th October 1535, the entire Scriptures were finished, and ready for printing. Coverdale was "helped" by the Latin and Dutch Bibles, as well as the portions which Tyndale had translated. But he calls his book "a special translation, not as a checker, reprover, or despiser, of other men's translations; but lowly and faithfully following his interpreters, and that under conviction." He had, in point of fact, as he says in his dedication to

* Westcott and Dr. Ginsburg.

MILES COVERDALE, BISHOP OF EXETER.

the king, five sundry interpreters; probably the German of Luther; the Swiss-German published at Zurich 1525–29; the Latin of Pagninus; the Vulgate: with the English Pentateuch, Book of Jonah, and New Testament of Tyndale. Having been abroad so long, his volume came, as Dr. Eadie says, "unheralded and unanticipated."

Mr. J. W. Whittaker, M.A., has shown that Coverdale translated from the Hebrew. And he says : "If the statement, translated out of Dutch and Latin, is in the original title-page, it contains a very great misrepresentation." Anderson concludes that these words were withdrawn by Coverdale himself, in 1536.

Coverdale's version shows a stronger sympathy with ecclesiastical words than Tyndale's; and is more rhythmical at the sacrifice of literality. For the prophetical writings he had no English guide, and he was swayed almost entirely, in this portion, by Leo Juda's Swiss-German Bible, a fact which partly accounts for the occasional obscurity of the Minor Prophets in our Authorised Version.*

Coverdale speaks of the adversity of those who were not only of ripe knowledge, but would also, with all their hearts, have performed that they begun, if they had not had impediment. It is of Tyndale, no doubt, that he chiefly speaks, who was now in prison, having gone as far with the Old Testament as 2 Chronicles.

The title is as follows :—" Biblia—the Bible, that is, the Holy Scripture of the Olde and New Testament, faithfully and truly translated out of the Douche and Latyn, into Englishe, MDXXXV. St. Paul, 2 Tessa. iii., 'Praie for us, that the Worde of God maie have fre passage and be glorified'; and St. Paul, Col. iii., 'Let the Worde of Christ dwell in you plenteously, in all wysdome'; and Joshua i. 'Let not the boke of this Lawe departe out of thy mouth, but exercyse thyselfe therein daye and nighte.'"

At the commencement of the dedication to Henry VIII., Coverdale alludes to the king's "dearest just wyfe and

* See *Quarterly Review*, vol. cxxviii. p. 318.

most vertuous pryncesse Queen Anne"; which he afterwards changed to "Queen Jane." And, of the existing
copies of the first edition, several are found made up with
the later dedication.

Mr. Fry has examined into this with his usual care.
The British Museum copy has "Anne," altered with the
pen into "Jane." The Bodleian has "Anne"; Sion
College has "Jane." And, in some copies the name of
the queen is expunged altogether. Lambeth Library has
an example of each. Those with the name "Jane," however, Mr. Fry found were from Nycholson's edition of
1537, a leaf of which had been inserted. Bibles are often
made up of two or three editions; frequent use, of course,
injuring them. Thus portions of the three editions of
Tyndale's New Testament, in quarto, 1536, are found in
the same volume. Mr. Fry sums up, after long comparison, that the leaf of the dedication to Queen Jane
is that of the edition of Nycholson, 1537. There is not
the least ground for supposing, with Lewis and Anderson,
that the publication of this first complete English Bible
was retarded, in order that the dedication to the king
might be reprinted with the name of Queen Jane.

The dedication has been described as fulsome. But
we must remember the circumstances under which it was
penned, and the real facts with which it deals. At the
commencement Coverdale compares the Pope to Caiaphas,
and then goes into Scriptural arguments against the
presumptions of the Papacy. He continues by asking
what is the cause of all these intolerable, and no more to
be suffered, abominations? Truly, even the ignorance
of the Scriptures of God. For how had it else been
possible that such blindness should have come into the
world, had not the light of God's word been extinct?
"How could men, I say, have been so far from the true
service of God, or from the due obedience of their Prince,
had not the law of God been clean shut up, depressed,
cast aside, and put out of remembrance? As it was before
the time of that noble king, Josias, and as it hath been also
among us, until your Grace's time, by whose righteous

administration (through the merciful goodness of God) it is now found again." And, later on, he says, in words which rise even to eloquence—"As false doctrine is the original cause of all evil plagues and destruction, so is the true executing of the law of God, and the preaching of the same, the mother of all godly prosperity. The only Word of God, I say, is the cause of all felicity; it bringeth all goodness with it; it bringeth learning; it gendereth understanding; it causeth good works; it maketh children of obedience; briefly, it teacheth all estates their office and duty. Seeing, then, that the Scriptures of God teacheth us everything sufficiently, both what we ought to do, and what we ought to leave undone; whom we are bound to obey, and whom we should not obey, therefore, I say, it causeth all prosperity, and setteth everything in frame, and, where it is taught and known, it lighteneth all darknesses, comforteth all sore hearts, leaveth no poor man unhelped, suffereth nothing amiss unamended, letteth no prince be disobeyed, permitteth no heresy to be preached, but reformeth all things; and why, because it is given by inspiration of God, therefore is it ever bringing profit and fruit, by teaching, by improving, by amending and reforming all them that will receive it, to make them perfect and meet unto all good works." In the close of this dedication certainly some strong language is used in reference to the part Henry had taken in opening the long-shut Word of God, but there is nothing which merits the charge of fulsomeness. Coverdale greatly rejoices that the Bible is no longer "clene shut up, depressed, cast aside, and put out of remembrance."

There is plenty of strong language also about the Pope. He is called the blind bishop of Rome, and blind Balaam. It is said that his hypocrites have taught people, instead of obeying prince and father and mother, to "step over father and mother's belly to enter into his painted religion." Strong language, and somewhat coarse! But we must remember that these were times when a king could be reminded of his "proper place," by being told by a priest, " your God is in my hand, and your wife at my feet." Coverdale is fond of alliteration, and speaks of " the Pope's pestilent picking of Peter's pence out of the kingdom," and his " deceiving with his devilish doctrines." He says that he uses " penance " and " repentance " indifferently, to show that the Reformers do not abhor the word " penance." Only it must be interpreted properly, being naught but " a very repentance, amendment, or conversion to God, and an unfeigned new creature in Christ, and to live according to God's law." In fact, Coverdale prefers to use different renderings; and says that more understanding of the Scriptures comes through various translations than any other way. The reader is by no means to be deceived by diverse expressions. And often there is no more diversity than between fourpence and a groat. Instead of cavilling, let the new boon of Scripture be thankfully received. He submits his translation to the king, but protests that he has neither wrested nor altered one word, for the maintenance of any manner of sect.

With reference to the " fulsomeness," Hume says, that no prince in Europe, not even the Pope himself in his own dominions, where he then united the civil and ecclesiastical powers, was possessed of such absolute authority as this headstrong Henry VIII. All parties vied with each other in paying him the most deferential submission, knowing that, though frank and generous, as Wolsey told Sir William Kingston, " rather than miss or want any part of his will, he would endanger the one-half of his kingdom." By this time, Henry had become irritable under the least opposition; and then, out came his ungovernable temper.

This being the first complete Bible printed in the English tongue, a somewhat particular account of it may be interesting to the reader. It was a handsome folio, as were all the Bibles at this early date. After the first leaf of the text, there follows a large woodcut, representing the six days' work of the creation; the chapter beginning with a large flourished letter, fourteen

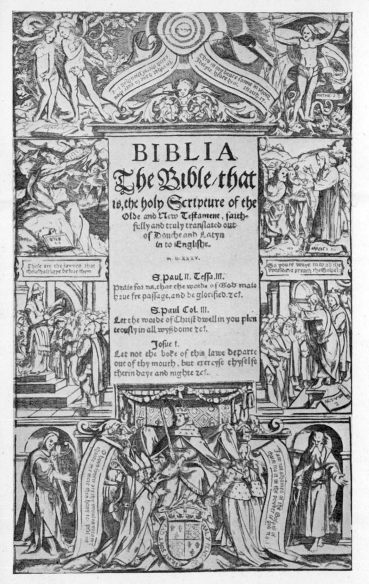

BIBLIA
The Bible that is, the holy Scripture of the Olde and New Testament, faithfully and truly translated out of Douche and Latyn in to Englishe.

M. D. XXXV.

S. Paul II. Tessa. III.
Praise for vs, that the worde of God maie haue fre passage, and be glorified. zc.

S. Paul Col. III.
Let the worde of Christ dwell in you plenteously in all wyssdome zc.

Josue I.
Let not the boke of this lawe departe out of thy mouth, but exercyse thyselfe therin daye and nighte zc.

TITLE TO THE FIRST ENTIRE ENGLISH BIBLE—COVERDALE'S, 1535.

lines of letterpress in depth.   At the end of Deuteronomy
is a folded map, headed " the description of the lande of
Promes, called Palestine, Canaan, or the Holy Lande."
The   third   part   ends   with   Solomon's   song, called
"Solomon's Ballettes"; and is followed by a title-page
saying, "All   the   prophetes   in   Englishe.   Esay   to
Malachy."   Then   comes   the   "Apocripha, the bokes
and treatises, which, amonge the fathers of olde are
not reckoned to be of like authoritie with the other
bokes of the Byble.   Nather are they founde in the
Canon of the Hebrue."   In a wooden border, the cuts
of the four corners being the four Evangelists, is "the
New Testament, the Gospell of St. Matthew, etc., to
Revalacion of St. Jhon."   The lower half of this page
contains " a faute escaped in prynting the New Testament."   And the imprint is as follows:—" prynted in
the yeare of our Lord MDXXXV., and fynished the
4th day of October."   On folio forty-one is a large cut
of the Tabernacle and its contents, which is repeated.
Each of the Gospels has a figure of the Evangelist pre-
fixed; that of St. Luke being repeated in the Acts of
the Apostles; and that of St. John in his first Epistle,
and in the Revelation.   To most of the Epistles of St.
Paul there is a cut showing the Apostle seated at a
desk writing, with a sword across his left arm, and a
weavers' loom to the left hand.   A synopsis precedes
every book.   There are also numerous quaint cuts, some
of them being frequently repeated.

The prologue to the whole is of considerable length.
Coverdale praises the Fathers for their love of God's
word, and their constant quotation of it in their works.
But, as soon as the Bible was cast aside, he says, and
every one began to write what came into his own head,
then grew the darkness of men's traditions.   And this
is the reason we have so many writers who seldom make
any mention of the Scriptures; or, if they do, the
reference is "so farre out of season, and so wide from
ye purpose, that a man may well perceave how that
they never sawe the oryginall."   He expresses his opinion

11

that, instead of several translations being harmful, there is more good to be got by comparing them together than from the glosses of sophistical doctors. This opinion has been acted upon in modern times; the English Hexapla being its product, where Coverdale's saying is printed on the title-page. A collation of the most important English Bibles was also made in 1847, by Mr. C. Roger of Dundee, and published by Messrs. Bagster & Sons.

Coverdale sometimes hits the meaning better than our present Authorised Version; as, for instance, in Prov. xxiii. 16, 17, our Version says, " Let not thine heart envy sinners; but be thou in the fear of the Lord all the day long. For surely there is an end; and thine expectation shall not be cut off." Coverdale renders the latter verse thus—" For the end is not yet come, and thy patient abiding shall not be in vain." He is, however, very paraphrastic, as, for instance, he translates the well-known verse, Prov. iv. 7, thus—" The chief point of wisdom is that thou be willing to obtain wisdom, and before all thy good to get thee understanding." Sometimes the semi-paraphrase is very simple and powerful, as witness the following:—" The same preacher was not wise alone, but taught the people knowledge also. He gave good hede, sought out the grounde, and set forth many parables. His diligence was to fynde out acceptable wordes, right Scripture, and the wordes of trueth. For the wordes of the wyse are like prickes and nales that go thorough, wherewith men are kept together, for they are given of one Shepherd onely. Therefore, beware (my sonne) that above these thou make thee not many and innumerable bookes, nor take dyverse doctrynes in hande, to weery thy body withal. Let us heare the conclucion of all thynges; feare God and kepe His commandements, for that toucheth all men; for God shall judge all workes and secrete thynges, whether they be good or evill " (Eccles. xii. 9–14).

Mr. Edgar thinks the term " Roundheads," so familiar a century later, may have been suggested by Coverdale's

Version. The passage is in 2 Sam. xiv. 25, which he renders:—

In all Israel there was not so fayre and so marvuelous goodly a man as Absalom. From the sole of his fote unto the toppe of his heade there was not one blemysh in him, and when his head was rounded (that was commonly every yeare, for it was too heavy for him, so that it must needs have been rounded) the heer of his heade weyed two hundred sicles after the Kynges weight.

Some other quaint renderings are:—

Psalm 51. 7.—Reconcile me with Isope, and I shal be clene.

Amos 7. 9.—The hye Hilchapels off Isaac must be layd waiste.

Acts 11. 29.—The disciples concluded to sende an hand reachinge unto the brethren that were in Jewry.

Rom. 9. 4.—Unto whom pertayneth the childshippe.*

All Tyndale's Prologues and Notes are omitted by Coverdale, as these had given the chief offence to the Catholics. The controverted passage in 1 John v., "There are three that bear record in heaven," is placed within a parenthesis, as are generally the additions to the original.

* *Bibles of England.*

CHAPTER XIV

FRESH LIGHT ON THE COVERDALE BIBLE

"Honours best thrive
When rather from our acts we them derive,
Than our foregoers."

SHAKESPEARE.

THE only perfect copy, including the title-page, now
known of this first printed English Bible, belongs to the
Earl of Leicester, and was discovered in 1846, concealed
under the false bottom of an old oak chest, in Holkham
Hall, near Walsingham. The book was formerly thought
to have been printed by C. Froschover, and the woodcuts
executed by Hans S. Beham ; to Froschover being assigned
the first place amongst the eminent printers of the day.
He carried on a successful trade, indeed, in this new art
of printing, for half a century. Mr. Fry, however, to
whom so much is owing in Biblical investigations, threw
doubt upon this, in his *Bible by Coverdale* ; and
equally doubted the title of Christian Egenolph, of
Frankfort, to be considered the printer. Mr. Batfield
inclines to him, indeed, and says that the book was
printed in the usual square Secretary Gothic type of
theological books executed abroad at this period, the
letters being angular Swiss or German. He says that
the dedication and address to the Christian reader were
afterwards added, by a London printer ; and that there
are 568 leaves, and 112 woodcuts.*

The truth has now probably been discovered, by Mr.
Henry Stevens, F.S.A., and is given at length in his
Bibles in the Caxton Exhibition, published in 1878.

* *First English Bible,* B. Batfield, M.A., F.R.S.

Mr. Stevens had spent twenty-five years, in "mousing and groping among old books of all sorts," as he tells us, when he came upon the truth, apparently by accident. His researches and comparisons of type, cuts, paper, water-marks, ink, and other printers' et-cetera, had all been vain and unprofitable. So that, he says, there was a thrill of delight when "the secret dropped into our open mouth of its own mere ripeness." To Jacob van Meteren, of Antwerp, must now be ascribed the honour of having printed the first entire English Bible that ever

HOLKHAM HALL, SEAT OF THE EARL OF LEICESTER, WHERE THE UNIQUE COVERDALE BIBLE IS PRESERVED.

saw the light. He may have assisted also in its translation, being a young man of position, and a good linguist. In his youth he had been taught the art of printing. And in his manhood he manifested great zeal in producing, at Antwerp, a translation of the Bible into English, "for the advancement of the kingdom of Christ in England," says his biographer; "and, for this purpose, he employed a certain learned scholar, named Miles Coverdale."

Jacob van Meteren was connected with the family of Abraham Ortelius, the geographer. After the printing,

Meteren found a very unexpected impediment to his publishing the complete bound work in Antwerp. The London bookbinders and stationers, finding the market filled with foreign books, usually at a cheap price, complained in 1533, and petitioned for relief. In consequence, an Act was passed, compelling foreigners to sell their editions entire, in sheets, to some London stationer; so that, at all events, the binders should not suffer. This new law came into operation at the beginning of the very year which saw the publication of this first printed English Bible. Consequently, Jacob van Meteren came to London to sell the edition; and he sold it probably to James Nycholson, of Southwark, who bought not only the entire edition, but the woodcuts, and probably the punches and type; so that all the copies of this Coverdale Bible have appeared in English binding.

Let, then, the name of Jacob van Meteren, of Antwerp, henceforth be held in honour in the records of "this art preservative of all arts." Towards the end of the reign of Edward vi., finding Antwerp no longer safe, on account of their religion, Meteren and his wife Ottilia resolved to remove to London, where they were invited by the king to settle. But, on their passage, the ship that bore them was attacked by a French cruiser, burned, and sunk.

Still further light has been thrown on the matter recently, however, by Mr. W. J. C. Moens, who has reprinted a document from an original copy in the old box of the Dutch Reformed Church, in Austin Friars. This was an affidavit, signed by Emanuel van Meteren, dated 28th May 1609, to the effect that he was brought to England in 1550 by his father, a furtherer of the Reformed Religion, and he that caused the first Bible "at his costes, to be Englisshed by Mr. Myles Coverdale, in Andwarp, the which his father, with Mr. Edward Whytchurch, printed both in Paris and in London." * This agrees with the statement of Simeon Ruytinck, on which Mr. Stevens relies; except the place of printing,

* Registers of the Dutch Reformed Church, Austin Friars, 1884, p. 14.

CHRISTOPHORUS FROSCHOVERUS

*Civis, Bibliopola et Typographus Figurinus
optime meritus.*

and the addition of the name Whitchurch, which may be a mistaken reference to the folio Bible of 1537. Mr. Stevens thought that Coverdale was simply, "the best proof-reader and corrector of his age." But it is probable that the translation was executed by him, at Antwerp, and that Van Meteren got the volume printed by some other printer, who may have been Froschover, of Zurich. Nycholson seems to have bought the copies for sale in England.*

The woodcuts and type were certainly not those used by Egenolph, of Frankfort. Dr. Ginsburg says, that he has in fact complete typographical proof that the Bible was printed by Froschover; and that Stevens's theory, about Jacob van Meteren being the real translator, and Coverdale only the corrector of the press, will not do at all. It is likely, however, that Meteren found the money for some of these early Bibles.†

Certain it is, that Henry VIII. received the Bible, and put it into the hands of the bishops, to peruse. After some delays, they redelivered the book; and, being asked by the king what they thought of it, they replied that it contained many faults. "Well!" said the king, "but are there any heresies maintained thereby?" They answered that there were no heresies that they could find. "If there be no heresies," said the king, "then, in God's name, let it go abroad among our people." For, in spite of the early action Henry had taken against the new doctrines, a change had been passing in his mind, as well as in the current of feeling around him. The tract, called the *Supplication of Beggars*, already referred to, had something to do with this, no doubt. It was scattered about the streets of London at night; and, the king's curiosity being excited, by the stories of its being "a marvel to hear of," he asked a merchant, named Elliot, to get one, and read it to him. It contained an attack on all the fraternity of Monks, Friars, and Pardoners; whose grasping spirit threatened to swallow

* Leslie Stephen.
† Westcott, 3rd edition,

up the whole country. " This is why," it said, " they will not let the New Testament go abroad in your mother tongue ; lest men should espy that they, by their cloaked hypocrisy, do translate thus fast your kingdom into their hands." The king listened patiently to every word ; and, when all was finished, said, as we have already seen, " If a man would pull down an old stone wall, and begin at the lower part, the upper part thereof might chance to fall on his head." Then, locking up the tract in his desk, he commanded all present not to disclose to any one that he had seen it.

The Apocryphal Books, with the exception of Baruch, were separated from the rest, with the following title :— " Apocripha ; the Bokes and Treatises which, amonge the fathers of olde, are not reckened to be of like authoritie with the other bokes of the Byble, nather are they founde in the Canon of the Hebrue." Coverdale hesitated somewhat as to making the separation ; and the prologue speaks doubtfully of their authority. But it required some courage, at that time, to make the distinction at all. And he was the first to do so, amongst the English Reformers. The distinction was made more decisively in Matthews' Bible, where they appear preceded by a valuable prologue, which formed part of Olivetan's Bible. And all the subsequent Protestant Bibles, down to the Authorised Version, continued to make them distinct from the inspired portion.

There was, however, either some neglect, or unavoidable delay, with regard to the sanction of this first printed English Bible, so that it was never properly sanctioned by either king or Parliament. The true history of the matter is given, at length, in the *Memorials of Myles Coverdale*, published by Bagster, in 1838. We may say, in a few words, that Cranmer and Cromwell, being strongly in favour of the vernacular Scriptures being given to the people, their general principles were also heartily promoted by Queen Anne Boleyn. When she was beheaded, on the 19th May 1536, everything came into contempt, for the time, which her name recalled.

The sanction already agreed upon, of Coverdale's Bible, was withdrawn; and nothing more was done in the matter. Henry, wavering very much on the subject, had only given his consent on the intercession of Queen Anne; and Foxe's copy of the injunctions in its favour was taken from one which was actually drawn up though never issued and acted upon. When the Queen's head fell, the injunctions were suppressed, and new ones published in their place.

A number of editions followed, however, without any formal sanction. And one of them, three years later, does not speak much for the honesty of the printer, Nycholson, of Southwark. There were so many blunders in it, that Coverdale remonstrated with him, and wished the copies bearing his name to be called in. Whereupon, Nycholson at once put to press another edition, of the same form and type, only substituting for Coverdale's the name of Johan Hollybushe. Undoubtedly, this first Bible was patronised, not only by Cranmer and Cromwell, but by Henry himself, though there was a good deal of vacillation on his part. We find Grafton, the printer, complaining, later on, that a post had come, ordering them to print, not "cum privilegio," but "ad imprimendum solum"; simply a license to sell what is set forth, without any evidence that it is the king's mind to set it forth. This letter concludes by hoping that the bishops will be as ready to read, as other men are to put the sacred writings forth. "For it is now seven years since the Bishops promised to translate and set forth the Bible, and as yet they have no leisure." *

Cranmer had much the same view of the small help to be obtained from the Bishops. Writing to Cromwell from Forde, a seaside retreat, a little way off Canterbury, and now a ruin for the occasional tourist from Herne Bay to explore, he asks him to obtain from the king, if he can, that the Bible which he sends may be sold and read of every person, without danger of any Act heretofore to the contrary, until such time as the Bishops shall set

* *State Papers*, vol. i. 1538.

forth a better, which will not be, in his judgment, till a day after doomsday. He encourages him, therefore, to suffer some snubs, slanders, lies, and reproaches for the same; which will be one day requited altogether.

Cranmer had been made Archbishop in 1533; and, as early as December, 1534, at a meeting of Convocation, it was agreed to request the king that a translation of the Scriptures should be made. In 1536 Cromwell's injunction was issued, for the whole Bible, in Latin and English, to be laid in the Choir. Coverdale's Bible was the only one then extant; and consequently it may, in a sense, be regarded as the first Authorised Version. Matthew's Bible, however, to which we must next turn, was taken up by Cranmer, and he procured its full authorisation. It is probable, therefore, that Coverdale's never came into use in the Churches; though his New Testament was printed from time to time.* Nycholson, of Southwark, printed it during the same year that Tyndale's New Testament, at last, got published in London.†

Coverdale's Bible has been called the Treacle Bible; Jeremiah viii. 22 being rendered, "Is there no treacle at Gilead?" also xlvi. 11, "Goe up unto Gilead, and bring treacle"; though many Bibles, in Henry VIII. and Elizabeth's reigns, repeated the word. Dr. Geddes preferred this version of Coverdale's to the Authorised. And there are certainly some very idiomatic renderings; of which we give a few :—

Psalm xc. 10.—The days of our age are three score years and ten.

Isaiah xlviii. 19.—Thy seed shall be like as the sand of the sea, and the fruit of thy body like the gravel-stones thereof.

Job xix. 18.—Yea, the very desert fools despise me.

Proverbs xvi. 28.—He that is a blabbe of his tongue maketh division.

* See *A Plea for Revision*, T. K. Abbott, M.A.
† By Berthelet. See *Quarterly Review*, vol. cxxviii,

Jeremiah xxii. 1.—Graven upon the edge of your altars, with a pen of iron, and with an adamant claw.

Exodus xx. 14.—Thou shalt not breake wedlocke.

Also, the dove returns with an olive leaf "in her nebb." David's "slaverings" run down his beard; their widows are neglected in the daily "hand-reachinge"; the earth shall "give a great crack"; and, he "wasteth his brayne" in foolish questions.

CHAPTER XV

COVERDALE'S LATER HISTORY AND OTHER WORKS

"What have we to do with time but fill it up with labour."
O. W. HOLMES.

COVERDALE had a very chequered career. We shall meet with him again; but we may here complete the chief biographical details about him. After Cromwell's execution (July 28, 1540), and Barnes's, he went to Germany, and became the pastor of a church at Bergzabern, near Strasburg; where he married the sister-in-law of Dr. M'Alpine, who helped to translate the first Danish Bible. He returned to England when Edward VI. came to the throne, and became one of his chaplains, and Almoner to the Queen Dowager, Catherine Parr, writing to Fagius from Windsor Castle, 21st October 1548. He preached at her funeral, in 1548, when he warned the people that the offerings then made were for the benefit of the poor, and the honour of the clergy, "not anything to profit the dead."

In 1551 Coverdale became Bishop of Exeter, succeeding Voysey, who resigned at last. But, on the accession of Queen Mary, he was deposed, imprisoned, and banished. A man of such prominence so long, he would not have escaped death, but for the intercession of the King of Denmark, Christian III., whose chaplain was Coverdale's brother-in-law. An evasive answer was returned to the king's first letter; but he wrote again, and saved Coverdale's life. It took a year to get him released from prison, on condition of his leaving the kingdom. Queen Mary alleged that he was in prison for a debt due to her in connection with his bishopric. The king availed himself of this to urge his release, as the more reasonable, inasmuch as he had cleared his accounts. It is interesting to see one translator helping another; his brother-in-law, the King of Denmark's chaplain, having been one of the translators of the recent Danish Version of the Scriptures.

Coverdale then lived for a while at Wesel, in Friesland, as pastor of an English congregation. After that he went again to Bergzabern; and finally to Geneva, where he was quite content to share in the production of the Genevan Bible; thus having a hand in four memorable versions. When Mary died, he returned to England again; but was not reinstated in his bishopric, as he had strong objections to the vestments still worn. From 1564 to 1566 he was Rector of St. Magnus the Martyr, London Bridge, but he was poor at the time of his appointment, after all his continental exile and wanderings, and wrote to Sir William Cecil that he might be excused the first-fruits. He says that he is not likely to live over a year; and, "if now, poor old Myles may be provided for, I shall think it as good as a feast." He preached after he had resigned his living, and Strype says that many ran after him. He died eighty-one years of age, even in those troubled times, in February 1569, and was attended to his grave in St. Bartholomew's Church, behind the Exchange, by vast crowds of those who admired and loved him.

Coverdale turned some of the Psalms into verse, and they were published with musical notes. We may give a single specimen (Psalm cxxxvii. 1, 2).

> "At the ryvers of Babilon,
>   there sat we down ryght hevely;
> Even when we thought upon Sion,
>   we wept together sorofully;
> for we were in soch hevynes,
> yt we forgat al our merynes,
>   and left of all our sport and playe.
> On the wilye trees yt were therby,
> We hanged up our harpes truly,
>   And morned sore both night and day."

This is amongst the earliest, if not the very earliest, attempts at a metrical version of the Psalms in our language. According to modern standards, it would only be called an attempt, but they soon became common after this. Queen Elizabeth versed the 25th Psalm; and Bacon's were published under the name of Theodore Basille.

A memorial tablet is erected to Coverdale, in the Church of St. Magnus, of which he was Rector. He was a faithful and painstaking man in all he put his hand to; and, during the short time of his bishopric at Exeter, Vowell says that he "most worthily did perform the office committed to him; he preached continually on every Holy Day; he was hospitable, liberal, sober, and modest; and his wife a most sober, chaste, and godly matron."* Coverdale knew German and Latin well, some Greek and Hebrew, and a little French. He was fairly read in theology; and, though not inclined to be a martyr, was a pious, conscientious, generous, and thoroughly honest and good man. As life went on, he became a stronger Puritan; and the Act of Uniformity brought down his reverend hairs with sorrow to the grave. A catalogue of twenty-eight works, with which he had more or less to do, is given by Leslie Stephen. And many of these were edited for the Parker Society, by the Rev. George Pearson, B.D., in two volumes. The authenticity of the portrait given is doubtful.

Many of Coverdale's works are translations; and amongst them is Luther's exposition of Psalm 23. Very touching it is, in parts, and Coverdale would have a strong fellow-feeling with the great Reformer, when he exclaims, in his comment on verse 5, "Thou preparest a table before me against mine enemies." "After this manner have I also, through the grace of God, behaved myself these eighteen years. I have ever suffered mine enemies to be wroth, to threaten, to blaspheme and condemn me, to cast their heads still against me, to imagine many evil ways, and to use divers unthirsty

* Catalog of Bishops of Exceter, 1584.

points. I have suffered them to take wondrous great thought, how they might destroy me and mine, yea, God's doctrine. Moreover, I have been glad and merry, and not greatly regarded their raging and madness, but have holden me by the staff of comfort, and had recourse to the Lord's table; that is, I have committed the cause unto God, wherein He hath so led me that I have obtained all my will and mind. And, in the meantime, have I done little or nothing, but spoken unto Him a Paternoster, or some little Psalm. This is all my harness, wherewith I have defended me hitherto; not only against mine enemies, but also (through the grace of God) brought so much to pass that, when I look behind me, and call to remembrance how it hath stood in the Papistry, I do even wonder that the matter is come so far. I would never have thought that the tenth part should have come to pass as it is now before our eyes. He that hath begun it shall bring it well to an end; yea, though nine Hells or Worlds were set on an heap together against it. Let every Christian man, therefore, learn this science; namely, that he hold him by this staff and sheephook, and resort unto this table, when heaviness or any other misfortune is at hand. And so shall he doubtless receive strength and comfort against everything that oppresseth him."

Another of Coverdale's works is the Confutation of Standish, in defence of Dr. Barnes's Protestation. They had been great friends at Cambridge, in the days when they met at the "White Horse," as we have seen. This work occupies more than a hundred pages in the large octavo edition of his works published by the Parker Society. Here he indignantly repels the charge of anti-nomianism, and exclaims, "The more I look upon your words, the more I wonder at your shameless slandering of the truth." Later on, he says, "Faith, then, neither destroyeth penance nor good works; but is the womb that beareth them both." *Penance* is constantly used where now we should say *Repentance*.

Coverdale exults in the conviction that, if Barnes were martyred, his words would prevail; and quotes his own

12

exclamation: "When I am dead, the sun and the moon, the stars and the elements, water and fire, yea, and also the stones, shall defend this cause, sooner than the verity should perish."

As to the outcry, that without the Church is no salvation; Coverdale says there are two Churches. "There is a congregation, church, and multitude, of froward and wicked doers, which not only gather themselves together, like roaring lions, fat bulls, wanton calves, and cur dogs, against Christ, as the 22nd Psalm complaineth; but also make laws, constitutions, statutes, ordinances, and traditions, against God's word; whereby it cometh to pass that, though they boast never so much of God's service, yet all is to them in vain, as the prophet, and Christ Himself, doth testify.   Another Church is there, which is the holy spouse, congregation, and company, of them that are of the fellowship of Christ, and walk not in darkness, but in the truth, having all their sins cleansed by His blood.   This Church continueth in the Apostles' doctrine, runneth not out from the heavenly fellowship of Christ and His members, distributeth the Sacraments duly and truly, ceaseth not from praying and well-doing, are of one mind and soul, and are glad to help one another.   The men of this Church pray in all places, lifting up pure hands.   In this Church is free pardon, and remission of sins for all true penitents."

As for the charge of heresy perpetually brought against the Reformers; the real heretics are those who have departed from the Word of God.   The heretics whom St. Paul prophesieth of (1 Tim. iv.) are such as, through their devilish doctrines, forbid men to live in holy wedlock, and command them to abstain from the meats which God hath created to be received of Christian men with thanksgiving.   The heretics of whom he speaketh in 2 Tim. iii. are such as, among all other vices, are covetous, boasters, proud, cursed speakers, false accusers, riotous, fierce, despisers of them that are good, traitors, having a shine of godly living, but denying the power thereof, resist the truth, being men of corrupt minds, and lewd in things pertaining to the faith. The heretics that he speaketh of in Acts xx. are such grievous wolves as spare not Christ's flock, and speak perverse doctrine to draw disciples after them. The heretics whom St. Peter speaketh of are such mockers as regard not God's promise; and are not only unlearned, but also unstable, and pervert Paul's Epistles, as they do the other Scriptures also to their own damnation. The heretics whom St. Jude speaketh of are such as, among other errors, are craftily crept into the Church, and turn the grace of God into wantonness, and deny God, the only Lord, and our Lord Jesus Christ; even such dreamers as defile the flesh, despise rulers, speak evil of the things that they know not; and, in such things as they know to be natural, do corrupt themselves as beasts, following the way of Cain, the error of Balaam for lucre's sake, and the treason of Core, feeding themselves, making feasts of other men's kindness, and having men in great reverence because of advantage. Have you not now well described the Papistry, and the unholy pillars of your unholy mother, the Church of the wicked? We thank you for pointing us to those Scriptures. We know you now, better than we did afore.

Much was made of Augustine's words, that he had not believed the gospel, but for the Church which gave it him. Franciscus Maronis, in the fourteenth century, with many others, had given this a meaning which Augustine never thought of, as if the Church could make new articles, by her own authority; and that people were bound to believe them, though not grounded in Scripture. Coverdale deals plainly with this, as his manner is; and, after showing how full of error Manicheus was, against whom Augustine was then writing; and that, in confuting him, he brought no other doctrine but the Scripture; he sums up: " By the circumstance, now, of Augustine's words, it is evident,—first, that he would believe no such doctrine as men brought up of their own heads; secondly, that he would believe no uncertain doctrine, nor that he knew not to be true; thirdly, that the occasion which moved him to believe the gospel, was the whole consent and authority of the universal Church. Now, like as he reporteth not of them, that they preached any other doctrine unto him, save the gospel; so saith he not that he believed any other learning, save only it."

Coverdale also translated *The Defence of a certain Poor Christian Man,* written in Germany, by "a right excellent and noble Prince." This also is well worth perusal, by those who would know how earnestly men contended for the faith once delivered to the saints in these days. Terms were constantly abused, and needed restoring to their true meaning. With regard to good works, after defending the true spiritual ones, the writer says : " Thou sayest we lack good works; but not such as come of love, or that Christ shall require of us at the Day of Judgment; but, to go a pilgrimage, to set up candles before images, to number up what we pray, to tell over a prayer of beads, to put difference in clothing, in meats, in prayers, in titles or names, where one had rather be called a Charter House monk, or a barefoot friar, than a Christian man. These, and such like slender and childish works, requirest thou of us. Which, though one had done them altogether, it were even as much as though he had ridden upon a stick, with boys in the street."

Mr. Fry has printed the 1535 edition of Coverdale's Bibles with a facsimile title from the Marquis of Northampton's copy; together with another leaf, in facsimile, from the Earl of Leicester's copy. In 1854 an original copy, nearly perfect, sold for £364.

Grindal was grieved that Coverdale was not made a bishop, when he returned to England, on Elizabeth's accession; for, he said, he was in Christ before them all.

As Dr. Cotton says, Coverdale has scarcely had justice done to him in Christopher Anderson's valuable work. Mr. Anderson was a Baptist minister in Edinburgh, and followed the Rev. J. Lewis, Vicar of Margate, who was the first to draw attention to the great interest attaching to our own English Bible, except Rev. A. Johnson, M.A., Rector of Swarkston, who published a pamphlet on the subject in 1730.

In the Caxton Exhibition, 1877, a number of the Coverdale Bibles were shown. And Mr. H. Stevens may well say, with regard to the Earl of Leicester's copy, and six others, all placed together—" Let no Englishman or American view these without first lifting his hat." Mr. Stevens says that Nycholson, the London printer, to whom all was sold, seems to have had as much trouble in working off his book as Simmons had in selling Milton's *Paradise Lost*; if we may judge by the number of new titles, and preliminary leaves, found in different copies. It is almost demonstrated that there was, originally, no dedication to the King. But towards the end of 1535, finding the Convocation, Cranmer, Cromwell, and the King more propitious towards free Scriptures than they had been, Nycholson probably got Coverdale to prepare the long and rather obsequious dedication to Henry VIII., to pave the way to a Royal Licence. The omission of the line—"and truly out of Douche and Latyn"—was simply a matter of the printer's taste and convenience ; Coverdale having more fully explained his authorities in his Epistles to the king and to the reader. Neither of the later editions, appearing directly afterwards, had the king's licence. Most likely, when Grafton obtained it for the Matthew Bible of 1537, a similar favour was granted to Nycholson, though it was too late. " Set forth with the Kinge's most gracious license" appears, however, in Nycholson's later quarto.

Coverdale appears to have had no monument as yet, but he is one of the eight immortals in the great window of the exquisite library at the London Guildhall.

I am indebted to Lord Peckover for the following quaint renderings from this memorable version :—

Isaiah 24. 9.—The beer shall be bitter.

Psalm 9. 20.—O Lord, set a scholemaster over them.

Prov. 27. 22.—Though thou shouldest bray a foole with a pestill in a mortar like otemeel.

Psalm 14. 1.—The foolish bodyes saye in their hertes, Tush! there is no God.

Prov. 23. 21.—He that is given to moch slepe shall go with a ragged cote.

Gen. 39. 2.—And the Lorde was with Joseph in so moch that he became a luckye man.

CHAPTER XVI

THE FIRST ENGLISH BIBLE FULLY AUTHORISED—
MATTHEW'S BIBLE

> " If life preserved for wife and children's sake,—
> If bliss which none but husbands, fathers, feel,—
> If worldly woe escaped, and worldly weal
>   Enjoyed, lands, houses, goods, with all to take
>   Captive the waverer,—had had power to shake
> Thy firm resolve, and quench thy fervent zeal,—
> Rogers, the Church had lost her earliest seal,
>   Stamped in thy heart's blood on the burning stake.
>   But nobler thought was thine, and loftier scope,
> The tempter's vile allurements to withstand
>   Victorious ; thine, the Christian's deathless hope ;
> The Christian's faith : and thus thy native land
>   Salutes in thee her harvest's firstling crop—
> In thee the Stephen of her martyred band."
>   Dr. MANT, Bishop of Down and Connor.

WE have seen that Tyndale's work was imperfect, and
that Coverdale's was not fully authorised, but very
shortly after Tyndale died, praying, "Lord, open the
King of England's eyes!" an English Bible was
sanctioned both by archbishop and king. It was
executed by John Rogers, one of Tyndale's converts,
who had been chaplain to the English congregation at
Antwerp, and had renounced the errors of the Church
of Rome. He took up the work where Tyndale left it
off, in 2 Chronicles, and revised Coverdale's version for
the rest of the Old Testament and the Apocrypha. His
only original translation appears to have been the prayer
of Manasses in the Apocrypha. For the New Testament
he took Tyndale's 1535 edition, revised the whole,
and added so many notes that his work is almost a
Commentary.

He only knew Tyndale a short time, but rapidly developed an ardent Protestantism. Tyndale was arrested in the spring of 1535, and Rogers had only arrived as chaplain to the merchant adventurers at the end of 1534. He proved the thoroughness of his conversion, however, like Luther, by taking a wife in the face of day! She was an Antwerp lady, without money, but "richly endowed with virtue and sobriety of life." Soon afterwards Rogers went to Wittenberg, to be the minister of a Protestant congregation there. Tyndale naturally handed over to him his incomplete translations. To conceal himself from the dangers which surrounded any one engaged in such labours, he adopted the fictitious name of Thomas Matthew, and the book has ever since been called Matthew's Bible. Possibly, however, Collier is right when he says that, as Tyndale lay under the imputation of unsound opinions, a further reason may have been to thus gain more general acceptance for it. He could not avoid a similar reputation, however, and in Queen Mary's Council Register, printed in Haynes's *State Papers,* there is an entry ordering John Rogers *alias* Matthew, to keep his house at Paul's, as a seditious preacher.* Certainly he could speak out, if that was what they meant, and he denounced the foul abuse of some of the money taken from the monasteries, making an outspoken protest before the Privy Council.†

The title was printed in red and black, within an elaborate wood engraving: "The Byble which is all the Holy Scripture, in whych are contayned the Olde and Newe Testament, truly and purely translated by Thomas Matthew. Essaye j 'Hearchin to ye Heavens and thou Earth geave eare: for the Lorde speaketh' MDXXXVII." At the foot of the page in a large bold letter is found— "Set forth with the Kinge's most graycious lycence."

The difference between the Pope and the new Head of the Church was thus seen in the most striking manner, the one shutting and the other opening. Rogers followed

* J. H. Blunt, *English Bible.*
† *John Rogers of Deritend.* R. K. Dent.

JOHN ROGERS, FIRST MARTYR IN QUEEN MARY'S REIGN.
FROM THE ORIGINAL IN THE HEROOLOGIA.

Tyndale very faithfully, but went over every sentence himself, having recourse to Hebrew, Greek, Latin, German, and English copies. The Prefaces and Notes were largely from Martin Luther. There is a table of principal matters, a gathering of certain hard words, and explanatory notes in the margin which would fill a good-sized volume. The whole production, indeed, indicated industry and thoroughness, and the table of principal matters extended over twenty-six folio pages, and combined the characters of a dictionary, a concordance, and a commentary. It was of great importance at such a time, as leading to an easy comparison of passages against such doctrines as the Sacrifice of the Mass; and, as appears by Bonner's Register, when the official prohibition of dangerous books was issued, in 1542, it was separated, with the notes, from the rest of the volume. It contained also an Epistle on the authority of the Apocrypha, extracted from the French Bible published in 1535 under the name of Olivetan, but really by Calvin.*

The Apocrypha were retained, indeed, probably in accordance with the publisher's wishes; but though notes appear numerously everywhere else, there are none here. Rogers took Coverdale's translation, just as he had left it, adding only a slight formal synopsis to each chapter, and making his preparatory protest against the inspiration of what he chose to call the " Hagiographa."

Westcott does not accept the identity of John Rogers and Thomas Matthew, but thinks that the latter was an unknown fellow-labourer.

The dedication was to the most noble and gracious King Henry the Eighth, King of England and of France, Lord of Ireland, Defender of the Faith, and under God the chief and supreme Head of the Church of England, and in it the translator says he was emboldened in his work by the way in which the king had suppressed superstition and maintained true holiness. He compares the neglect of the Old Testament in ancient Jewish times to that of

* This was also included, almost unaltered, in Cranmer's Bible of 1540. See *The Bible in the Church*, Westcott.

the entire Scriptures of late, and trusts that, as Hezekiah and Josiah did honour to them, the King of England to-day will equal or surpass them.

Two short examples, embracing familiar passages, will show the variations from the present version, and the peculiar orthography of this translation.

GENESIS. ¶ *The fyrst Chapter.*

In the beginnyng God created heauen and erth. The erth was voyde and emptye, and darcknesse was vpon the depe, & the spirite of God moued vpon the water.

Than God sayde : let there be lyght : & there was lyght. And God sawe the lyght that it was good : & deuyded yᵉ lyght from the darcknesse, & called the light the daye, & the darcknesse the nyght : and so of the euenyng & mornyng was made the fyrst daye.

JOHN. ¶ *The fyrst Chapter.*

In the beginnynge was the worde, & the worde was with God : and the worde was God. The same was in the beginnynge wyth God. All thinges were made by it, and wythout it, was made nothynge that was made. In it was lyfe, & the lyfe was the lyght of men, & the lyght shyneth in yᵉ darcknes, but the darcknes comprehended it not.

I am indebted to Lord Peckover for the following renderings :—

Deut. xxxiv. 7.—And yet hys eyes were not dym nor his chekes abated.

Judges v. 12.—Up, up, Debora. Up, up, and synge a songe | up Barak and take thy praye.

1 Sam. iii. 13.—For the wickednesse whych he knoweth how his sonnes are ungraciouse | and he was not wroth therewith.

1 Sam. xviii. 6.—Women came out of all cyties of Israel syngyng and daunsing agaynst Saul | with tymbrelles | with joye | and with fydelles.

2 Kings ix. 30.—Jezebel starched her eyes.

Here is a sample of the notes. 2 Kings. ii. 23—the mockers of Elisha :—

" The contempt of godly men, chiefly preachers, is an offence most grievous, whose authority ought to be most holy and reverent to all the people, whom he that receiveth or againsaieth receiveth or rejecteth God. Fathers while they correct not the wantonness of their children, while they hold them not under nurture, while they suffer them to jest and scoff with every man, and let them attempt everything unpunished, the Lord punisheth them with the children in many ways."

Here is another example of the notes :—

Psalm i.—" To stand in judgment is to win the process, and to have sentence pronounced on their sides ; as to rob judgment is to let the process, and to have sentence pronounced against right or truth. So then this text meaneth no more but that the wicked shall have such a terrible sentence given upon them that they shall not be able to abide when the Lord shall come to the general judgment ; it meaneth not that the wicked shall not appear in the judgment."

The book was published by Grafton and Whitchurch in 1537, and forwarded at once to Cranmer. It was really a private speculation of Grafton, the printer, and well it might be, as book after book was issuing from the press, and still the book of God was only " made in Germany."

Grafton was a citizen and grocer in London, and a man of good family. His publications appear to have ceased in 1553, but he wrote some works after that, and *Grafton's Chronicle* was published in 1569. His device was a pun, as was not uncommon in those days, though to us the wit seems small. It was a tun, with a fruit-tree issuing from the bung-hole, indicating *graft tun*. He was twice master of the Grocers' Company, was in Parliament more than once, and became master of Bridewell. In later life, however, he was reduced to poverty, and we find him, after 1570, proposing to become a public informer.

Whitchurch appears to have been originally a

merchant, and his connection with Grafton was dissolved in 1541, his latest extant publication being dated 1560. He lived first at the Well and Two Buckets in St. Martin's-le-Grand, and last at the Sun in Fleet Street. He married the widow of Cranmer, who survived him.

Cranmer was very pleased when the book was sent to him, and it was through his and Cromwell's influence that it received royal sanction.

He writes to Cromwell, from his quiet country-house at Forde, not far from Herne in Kent, where Ridley was vicar, and had the Te Deum in English for the first time:—

"My very singular good Lord.—In my most hearty wise I commend me unto your Lordship. And whereas I understand that your Lordship, at my request, hath not only exhibited the Bible which I sent unto you, to the King's Majesty, but also hath obtained of His Grace, that the same shall be allowed by his authority, to be bought and read within this realm; my Lord, for this your pains, I give you my most hearty thanks, assuring your Lordship you have showed me more pleasure here than if you had given me a thousand pounds; and I doubt not but that hereby such fruit of good knowledge shall ensue, that it shall well appear hereafter what high and excellent service you have done unto God and the king, which shall so much redound to your honour that, besides God's reward, you shall obtain a perpetual memory for the same within this Realm.

At Ford, the 13th day of August 1537,

Your own boundman ever,

T. CANTUARIEN."

In another letter, at the end of the same month, he said that this deed he should hear of at the great Day, when all things should be opened and made manifest.

Grafton wrote to Cromwell the same month, asking to have it licensed under the Privy Seal, and later on that he should have the sole printing of it. This was because the Dutch were so ready to print for mere gain, and did it incorrectly.

CHAPTER XVII

BISHOP BECKE'S BIBLE

"Bibles laid open, millions of surprises."
HERBERT.

In 1551 a Bible was published under the name of
Bishop Becke, which was almost a reprint of Matthew's.
It was said of him:

"A prince of the publicans, a taker of tolls,
Is become a preacher, a feeder of souls."

He published it in a handsome though a cheaper form,
and dedicated it to the young king, Edward VI., whom he
lectures on his duties. If people would spare an hour a
day for reading it, he says, they would soon abandon
blasphemy, swearing, carding, and dicing; they would
put away all pride, prodigality, riot, licentious, and dis-
solute living.

In this Bible, Psalm xci. 5 is translated " any bugges by
night." It has been thought that the translator may
have meant "bogies," which perhaps is a little nearer the
suggestion of terror, though there might be a difference
of opinion on that. Coverdale's and Taverner's also have
" bugs."

Many of Becke's notes are objectionable. They are
also often very long, and are printed in the same type as
the text. Those to Matthew vi. occupy nearly one and a
half columns, and are practically a sermon on the Lord's
Prayer. The notes to Matthew xix. are indecent, and
there is much abuse of the Church, her doctrine, and her
clergy. Here is a sample of Annotations which were
disapproved at the time and never reprinted :—

1 Pet. iii.—" He dwelleth wyth his wyfe according to knowledge, that taketh her as a necessarye healper, and not as a bonde servaunte or a bonde slave. And yf she be not obedient and healpfull unto hym endeavoureth to beate the feare of God into her heade, therby she maye be compelled to learne her dutie, and to do it."

There are a number of woodcuts resembling those in Flemish and other Bibles printed about that time, and they are explained by such doggerel as the following :—

" By the Stars in hys hand we may wel se
  What manner of men our preachers should be."

" The open enemye is most oughly in syghte,
  But the wolfe in the Lambe's skyne doeth all the spight."

" The elect of God onely can singe the songe
  That soundeth on the herte, and not on the tonge."*

To return to the original Matthew's Bible.

Tyndale had just been martyred and his translation condemned and denounced, and yet here it was under the highest sanction. For it was practically very much the same thing, and it was brought out by his convert and friend. Well may Mr. Edgar say :

" The licensing of Matthew's Bible was enough to have waked the ashes of Tyndale into laughter. Matthew's Bible was just a revised edition of Tyndale's translations, which had been so fiercely denounced, with a new part, from Ezra to Malachi, added. How little do some people know what they condemn and what they commend." †

Before Henry died, however, thirty-one impressions of the original Matthew's Bible had been issued, but no reign presents greater contrasts than this. At one time it was a criminal offence to teach children the Lord's Prayer in English; at another the entire Bible was ordered to be placed in every parish church. It has been generally supposed that Henry's private sentiments were in favour of the free circulation of the Scriptures, but his

* *Old Bibles*, Dore.   † *Bibles of England*.

chief concern was always to secure and strengthen his own absolute authority. He was fickle and capricious, continually wavering to and fro, so that the Reformers could never reckon on his protection for a single day. No man could foretell in the evening what would be the royal will and the National Creed the next morning. There was a royal proclamation against the writings of Coverdale, Tyndale, Luther, and Melanchthon in the last year of his reign, which repeated much the same prohibition as had been issued in 1539. When the solemn and precise Charles V. abdicated, it suited his humour to turn clock-maker, and, discovering that scarcely any two clocks went exactly alike, he wondered that he had expected all his subjects to agree. It was Henry VIII.'s fixed determination, however, to make every one in England agree with him both on social and ecclesiastical questions. At the same time, as Froude says, no trimmer ever did any great work in the world, and offensive in the last degree as many of his characteristics were, it was such a man that could strike the roots of the Reformation deep into English soil.* In estimating him also, let not the bright figure of his early days be forgotten. Bright it is as we see him in everything the people's friend; kneeling with them at St. Paul's and Westminster; fighting openly at the Tilt; maying at Greenwich with pasteboard Gogs and Magogs; a scholar able to discuss with bishops and priests the New Testament of Erasmus; everywhere seen and yet never to be trifled with. He was, indeed, such a people's head as England had never had, and has not since possessed. And if his later life makes us cry out "O mores!" we must also with a special emphasis cry "O tempora!"

However, Bibles became multiplied in spite of the fickleness of both monarch and people, and able men were raised up to advocate their reading. There is a famous story of how honest Hugh Latimer handled a

---

* The world owes some of its greatest debts to men from whose very memory it recoils, and the worst cause has often been illustrated with the most heroic virtue.—STUBBS.

13

friar at Cambridge in 1529, soon after his conversion. The friar, a prior of the Black Friars, called Buckingham, preached a sermon in which he attempted to show that the Bible was so full of obscurities that it was not safe to give it to the people. He said that, when the plough-man hears in the New Testament, "No man having put his hand to the plough and looking back is fit for the kingdom of God," he might in panic cease from the plough ; that the baker might give us no leavened bread on hearing that "a little leaven leaveneth the whole lump"; and also that the simple man, when he hears "if thine eye offend thee, pluck it out and cast it from thee," might blind himself, and soon the world would be filled with beggars. On the same afternoon Latimer replied to the friar, who sat right opposite with a malicious scowl, anticipating a triumph. But with his ready knowledge of the Word of God, the Reformer showed the clearness with which its great truths were usually revealed, so that he that ran could read, and then, as for the figurative language, he said, it was easily understood by the common sense of mankind. "For example," said he, looking full at the friar, "when painters picture to us a fox preaching out of a friar's cowl, none is so mad as to take this to be a fox that preacheth, but knows well enough that the painting represents what hypocrisy, craft, and subtle dissimula-tion lieth many times hid in these friars' cowls, willing us to beware of them."

CHAPTER XVIII

HONEST HUGH LATIMER

"Amid my list of blessings infinite
Stands this the foremost, that my heart hath bled."

YOUNG.

YES, there was some hard hitting in these days, and another extract from Latimer is pertinent to our subject. It is from the famous Plough Sermon preached in the Shrouds of St. Paul's, and he says, as we have partly seen :

"Where the devil is resident, and has his plough going, then away with books and up with candles; away with Bibles and up with beads; away with the light of the gospel, and up with the light of candles—yea, at noon-day. Where the devil is resident, that he may prevail, up with all superstition and idolatry, censing, painting of images, candles—a new service of men's inventing—as though man could find a better way to honour God with than God Himself hath appointed."

It is strong language, but did not the state of the country, after so long a night, justify it! Imagine, for instance, the following conversation between a vicar and his bishop. The vicar is Thomas Forret, Vicar of Dollar, whose eyes had been opened after a visit to Cologne, and who used to commit three chapters of the Bible to memory every day, and repeat them to his servant at night. It was in 1538 that his bishop—Crighton (or Creighton) of Dunkeld—accused him of "heresy" for preaching every Sunday on the Epistle and Gospel for the day amongst other things, and when he appeared the bishop said, "My joy, Dean Thomas, I am informed that you preach the Epistle and Gospel every Sunday to your parishioners. It is too much to preach every Sunday, for in so doing you make the people think that we should preach likewise. It is enough for you, when you find any good Epistle or good Gospel that setteth forth the liberties of Holy Church, to preach that, and

HUGH LATIMER, BISHOP OF WORCESTER.

let the rest alone." The vicar answered, "I think, my Lord, that none of my parishioners will complain. Your Lordship saith it is too much to preach every Sunday. I think it is too little, and I wish your Lordship did the like." Crichton: "Nay, nay, Dean Thomas, we were not ordained to preach." Forret: "Your Lordship directs me when I meet with a good Epistle, or a good Gospel, to preach upon it. I have read both the Old and New Testament, but have never met with a bad Epistle or a bad Gospel. But if your Lordship will show me which are the bad and which are the good, I will preach on the good, and let the bad alone." Crichton: " I thank my God I know nothing of either the Old or New Testament; therefore, Dean Thomas, I will know nothing but my portass (breviary) and my pontifical. Go away and lay aside these phantasies, or you will repent it when too late." * He was burned on the Castle Hill at Edinburgh.

Latimer was a Cambridge man, a Bachelor of Divinity, and a Fellow of Clare. He bore the cross in processions for the University, and attacked Melanchthon when he took his B.D. But he had an honest mind, and when Bilney chose him as confessor, after his attack on the German Reformer, he gained Latimer over to his own views, and he never went back from them, though he was in prison for years in Henry's reign, and lit the famous candle in Queen Mary's. He joined the group who met at the " White Horse," which was called " Little Germany."

In 1530 he sat with some fellow-commissioners who deprecated the publication of the English New Testament, but he soon saw what a mistake he had made, and wrote a letter to the king urging it. He said afterwards he would be guided solely by God's book, and rather than dissent one jot from it, would be torn by wild horses. Seldom has there been such plain speaking as Latimer's, and when he addressed the Convocation (*Ad Clerum*, 1536) he imagined Christ saying to them:

"You preach very seldom, and when you do preach, do nothing but cumber those that preach truly. I would that Christian people should hear my doctrine, and at their convenient leisure read it also. Your care is not that all men may hear it, but all your care is that no layman do read it."

* *Acts and Monuments*, Persecution in Scotland.

There is a valuable *Life of Rogers*, by Mr. J. Lemuel Chester, published by Longmans. He was the proto-martyr in Queen Mary's reign, and the deadly persecutions of that time of blood could not have commenced with an example more likely to tend to the permanent downfall of Popery in the land. For Rogers was a saint, a scholar, a gentleman, and a public benefactor. The only crimes ever urged against him were that he believed in the doctrine of the early English Church, and translated the Word of God to show that this was scriptural, and for the general edification of the people, who had been in darkness so long. His portrait shows what manner of man he was, and his son, Daniel Rogers, had the character of being one of the most accomplished gentlemen of the time in Queen Elizabeth's reign. We shall meet with him again, and will only emphasise now that he was the first to give to the English people both a Commentary and a Concordance. Where this first "Authorised Version" was printed is not known, but it was at the expense of Grafton and Whitchurch, who may be called the publishers. It came out in August 1537, and is evidently of foreign workmanship. Antwerp, Hamburg, and Lubec have been named, and Dr. Cotton gives the preference to the last, on the ground that the two large fine wood engravings, the title, and Adam and Eve, are struck from the blocks which had been used in a Dutch Bible. Only the publishers were English.

No doubt Matthew's Bible had a mighty influence in the nation at large, and as one illustration of it we may refer briefly to Marbeck, one of the Windsor Protestants. He made a Concordance for himself, at great labour, and when under examination was asked what help he had from others. "I will tell your Lordship," he answered the Bishop of Salisbury, "what instructor I had to begin it. When Thomas Matthewe's Bible came first out in print, I was much desirous to have one of them; and being a poor man, not able to buy one of them, I deter-mined to borrow one amongst my friends, and to write it forth. And when I had written out the five books of

PLACE OF MARTYRDOM, SMITHFIELD.

Moses in fair great paper, and was entered into the Book of Joshua, my friend Master Turner (Magdalen College, Oxford) chanced to steal upon me unawares, and seeing me write out the Bible, asked me what I meant thereby. And when I had told him the cause, 'Tush,' quoth he, 'thou goest about a vain and tedious labour. But this were a profitable work for thee, to set out a Concordance in English.'" Well might the Bishop of Hereford, one of his examiners, say, after looking over a quire or two of his work, "This man hath been better occupied than a great sort of our priests."

When Gardiner, Bishop of Winchester, examined this man in his own house, he examined him in his own way, which was as follows :—

"What a devil made thee to meddle with the Scriptures ? Thy vocation was another way, wherein thou hast a goodly gift if thou didst esteem it ?" Foxe's note on this is that Christ says "Search the Scriptures," and Winchester says that the devil makes men to meddle with the Scriptures. However, Marbeck answered, "I do esteem it; and have done my part therein according to that little knowledge that God hath given me." "And why the devil," quoth the bishop, "didst thou not hold thee there ?"

Another of these notable Windsor Protestants was Henry Filmer, who was churchwarden. One of the suppressed friars was made vicar, but still had his friar's heart, and brought his friar's tales into the pulpit. Once he said that "Our Lady held out her breasts to St. Bernard, and spouted her milk into his eyes," whereupon Filmer went to him and protested against his rubbish. In the end, right under the towers of Windsor Castle, three such men were burnt to death together, Marbeck just escaping. It was rather natural that one of them, Anthony Pearson, should say that many of the bishops of the day were bite-sheeps instead of bishops. When Pearson came to the place of execution, he embraced the stake with a cheerful countenance, and, kissing it, said, "Now welcome, mine own sweet wife ! for this day shalt thou and I be married together in the love and peace of God."

Such abominable persecution took effect even over the water, and soon afterwards Ralph Hare was brought up before Gardiner at Calais. He was charged with " many heinous and detestable errors, namely, that he was a great reader of the New Testament in English; that he was such an one that indeed neither used to take holy bread, holy water, holy ashes, nor holy palm." But they could not deny that he lived a holy life. In fact, at Calais there was a great deal of persecution, but they found it difficult to answer the supposed heretics. One of them, William Button, asked a friar who pretended to deliver souls out of Purgatory, whether the Pope could do it. " There is no doubt of that," said the friar. " Why, then, doth not he out of charity deliver all the souls thereout ? " And he turned to Dr. Darly, the commissary, and said, " If your holy father the Pope may deliver souls out of Purgatory, and will not of charity deliver them, then I would to God the king would make me Pope, and I would surely deliver all out without money."

Such persecutions were miserably frequent, and we give these as examples, and pass on. Foxe exclaims once, " Why stand I here numbering the sand ! " But he is able to add, " Yet, nevertheless, so mighty the power of God's Gospel did work in the hearts of good men that the number of them did nothing lessen for all this violence and policy of the adversaries."

It was the strong Protestant character of some of the notes that led to Matthew's Bible being so soon superseded by the Great. But was there not a cause ? Think of Tyndale's bishop in Gloucestershire being an Italian who had never set foot in his diocese ! All he wanted was the money, and well may Matthew exclaim, in his note on 1 Tim. iii. 1—

" If a man covet the office of a Bysshoppe he desyreth a good work. This Bysshoppe is a sear to, a taker heade to, or an oversear ; which when he desyreth to feade Christes flock with the fode of healeth, that is, with his holy

worde, as the Bysshopes did in Paul's tyme, desyreth a
good worcke, and the very office of a Bisshope.   But he
that desyreth honoure ; gapeth for lucre ; thirsteth great
rentes ; seketh preeminence, pompe, dominion ; coveteth
abundance of all thinges without want, rest and hertes
ease, castells, parks, lordshyppes, yerldomes, etc., desyre
not a worcke, moch lesse a good worcke."

CHAPTER XIX

THE GREAT BIBLE

YES, as we have often seen, what we now call Protestantism is the ancient religion of the British Isles. Those who first brought the Gospel to England, St. Patrick in Ireland, and St. Columba in Scotland, walked in the truth. If the Protestant is asked, "Where was your religion before the Reformation?" the countryman's retort stands good, "Where was your face this morning before it was washed?" The Pearl of great price was hidden with trash and filth, and our Reformers removed only what obscured it. The Church was known to be the Spouse of Christ by her first features and complexion, though she cast off the new Italian dress. Christianity was obscured like the sun under the cloud, but still the sun was the same, and at length conquered the mists. "'Tis a fine question to ask where the sun was before noonday?" So says the *Charge of Novelty*,* ending with, "he that will prefer an old disease before a new cure, let him be ever sick. Where did your Church lurk, in what cave of the earth slept she after so many hundreds of years together, before the birth of Martin Luther? The reply is that she lurked beneath the folds of that garment of many colours which the hand of superstition had woven and embellished for her, and wherewith she was fantastically encumbered and disguised. She slept in that cavern of enchantment where costly odours and intoxicating fumes were floating around to overpower her sense, and to suspend her faculties; till at last a voice was heard to cry, *Sleep no more*. And then she started up, like a

* London, 1683.

TITLE-PAGE OF THE GREAT BIBLE, 1539.

strong man refreshed, and shook herself from the dust
of ages. Then did she cast aside the gorgeous things
which had oppressed her, and stood before the world a
sacred form of brightness and purity." *

It was a very difficult matter to get released, however,
and the credit of it must never be put down too much to
Henry VIII. The determined elements of his character
were a strong point in the whole business indeed, but the
work was very largely in the hands of other and different
men. The way in which Luther handled him, exposing
his royal ignorance and vanity, though it stung him at
the time, did not materially alter his course. "What
most surprises me is," wrote Luther, "not the ignorance
of this Hal of England; not that he understands less
about faith and works than a log of wood; but that the
devil should trouble himself to make use of this man
against me, when he knows that I don't care a straw for
either one or the other. King Henry justifies the
proverb, 'Kings and princes are fools.' Who sees not
the hand of God in the blindness and imbecility of this
man! I shall say very little more about him at present;
for I have the Bible to translate and other important
matters to attend to." In fact the king's book, though
so heartily welcomed by the Pope, and gaining for him
the title of Defender of the Faith, contained little of
either thought or research, and was possibly written for
him in part. Luther laughs at him and plays with
him finely, being fresh from victory. He went too far
indeed, and afterwards apologised for such strong language.
In the Preface to this same Great Bible it is said:
"The Bishop of Rome conferred on King Henry VIII. the
title of Defender of the Faith, because His Highness
suffered the Bishops to burn God's Word, the root of
Faith, and to persecute the lovers and ministers of the
same."

Yes, and the people suffered all this, for at this period
they voluntarily rushed into slavery, as Tacitus tells us
the Romans did in the reign of Tiberius.

* See Le Bas, *Life of Wycliffe.*

Bishop Warburton looks more deeply into these things than most when he says :

"Generally some oblique passion gratifies itself in decrying the grosser corruptions supported by and supporting those it hates. The machine thus set a-going, truth has fair play ; she is now at liberty to procure friends, and to attach them to her service. This was the course of things in the Revolution in Henry VIII.'s reign, and is the natural rise and progress of religious reformations in general. For if in the state of such established error, Providence was to wait till a love of truth had set men upon shaking off their bondage, its dispensations could never provide that timely aid which we now find they always do to distressed humanity. And it is knowing as little of the religious as of the moral course of God's Providence to upbraid those who have profited of this blessing with the baseness of the instruments that procured it."

We come, then, now to the *Great Bible,* and the work of Cromwell and Cranmer in connection with it. There had been an attempt made by Cranmer four years previously (1534) to get a translation executed by the bishops, but their entire co-operation could not be secured. The matter was brought up in Convocation, and the king asked that a right translation might be prepared. The work was divided out, but Bishop Stokesley returned his "paper book," and refused to have anything to do with it, as likely to infect the people with heresy. Whereupon the chaplain to the Duke of Norfolk said, "I can tell your Grace why my Lord of London will not bestow any labour or pains this way. Your Grace knoweth well that his portion is a piece of the New Testament. But he, being persuaded that Christ has bequeathed him nothing in his Testament, thought it madness to bestow any labour or pains where no gain was to be gotten, and, besides this, it is the Acts of the Apostles, who were simple poor fellows, and therefore my Lord of London disdained to have to do with any of them."

This Stokesley was the "natural brute beast," who, when he was lying at the point of death, rejoiced that in his lifetime he had burned fifty heretics. What is the "conscience" capable of, when seared as with a hot iron, and in fact an old man of our own time said he had lived long enough to hear men attempt to justify nearly every crime, except murder. Hall says he was a man of great wit and learning, but of little discretion and humanity.

The bishops protested in 1531 against the reflections upon them in the Prefaces to the new translations. But they did not set to work to prepare a "sound translation," as the King then urged them to do. For, as Froude says, the work of the Reformation was not much furthered by the official clergy. It was largely done by volunteers from the ranks, and forced upon the Church by the secular arm. "The stream flowed on, caring little for human opposition. To swim with, or to swim against it, affected little the velocity with which the English world was swept into the new era."

In fact, to change the figure, we are often reminded of Lord Bacon's remark, that in human affairs great weights often hang on small wires.

14

CHAPTER XX

" In this Act was laid the foundation stone on which the whole later history of England, civil as well as ecclesiastical, has been reared, and the most minute incidents become interesting, connected with an event of so mighty moment."

FROUDE, on the publication of the *Great Bible.*

So the Great Bible was no bishop's work, but a further revision of Matthew's Version by Miles Coverdale, Cromwell instigating and supporting the whole undertaking. Cromwell was practically Wolsey's successor, having formerly been his secretary. His love of the Scriptures had been shown early, and it is said he had committed most of Erasmus's Latin Testament to memory. He often used to tell his friends, however, what a ruffian he had been in his youth, and it did not seem likely that he would become the great exposer of Papist juggleries, bringing the Rood of Grace to St. Paul's Cross to be torn to pieces by the people, proving the blood at Hales to be duck's blood, and the " holy maid of Kent " to be a worthless character. In fact, he was rather a zealous Papist in his early irreligious days—a combination of opposites always possible. If we may believe the story, it seems that the people of Boston, Lincolnshire, resolved to send to Rome for a renewal of their two pardons, and accordingly dispatched two men with the proper writing, and requisite money. Coming to Antwerp, where Cromwell then was, and the courage of one of them failing, they prevailed on Cromwell to accompany them, which he did, being fond of travel and adventure. Arriving in Rome, and finding the Pope was fond of delicacies, he prepared some fine

THOMAS CROMWELL.
Earl of Essex.

Holben Pinx.   I.Absolon sculp.

In the Possession of
Edward Southwell Esqr.

dishes of jellies, never before seen there, and choosing his
time when the Pope had come in from hunting, and gone
into his pavilion, he brought his presents, with " three men's
song," as it was then called. The Pope, surprised and
pleased with the song, and understanding that they were
Englishmen, and did not come empty-handed, called them
in ; whereupon Cromwell, doing his obeisance, offered him
his jelly junkets. Upon a cardinal's tasting and recom-
mending them, the Pope tried them, and was so much
pleased with them that he granted them their request,
and commanded them to teach his cook the art of making
the dishes. Cromwell made several confections in later
life that were not so palatable.

He certainly became one of the chief promoters of the
open English Bible, and amongst the last things he did
was to father the one ordered to be placed in every
church, and commonly called the Great Bible. The idea of
Coverdale's earlier Bible was not satisfactory, and
Matthew's notes were highly controversial, and sure to
provoke great opposition. Cromwell went to Coverdale
about the matter, in the early part of 1538, and got him
to undertake a new edition on the basis of Matthew's, but
to be issued without his notes, and with a more complete
collation of the Hebrew and Latin Texts. Coverdale
undertook it at once, and spent about a year on the work.
He " set in a private table the diversity of readings of all
Texts, Hebrew, Chaldee, Greek, Latin, with such Annotations in another table as shall doubtless elucidate and
clear the same, as well without any singularity of opinions
as all checkings and reproofs." He was quite willing to
take another man's work as the basis of his own, but the
alterations he made were numerous. He was not a press-
corrector, but an editor, and one valuable work, just
published, had a very important influence on the version
he now produced. This was a new Latin version of the
Old Testament with the Hebrew Text, and a Commentary
chiefly from Hebrew sources, published by S. Munster in
1534–35. It was a valuable addition to his critical stories,
and, according to Westcott, the Old Testament may indeed

be said to be chiefly a revision of Matthew's by the aid of Munster. And what Munster was to the Old Testament, Erasmus was to the New. His Latin version frequently led to the giving up of Tyndale's renderings, in the 1534 text.

There are some idiomatic renderings in the Great Bible, as, for instance, when Christ is said to be in the midst of the Doctors in the Temple, "hearinge them and posinge them." In the Temptation also Satan is said to show Christ all the kingdoms of the world " in the twynklelynge of an eye." In Psalm cxxxii. 4 we have " neither the temples of my head to take any rest." There is quite a love of variety in the translation, " the chief musician" in the Psalms being sometimes "the chanter," and sometimes " he that excelleth."

I am indebted to Lord Peckover for the following illustrations :—

Gen. 43. 34.—And they drinking were dronke with him.

Lev. 19. 27.—Ye shall not rounde the lockes of your heades, neyther shalte thou marre the tufles of thy bearde.

Deut. 32. 10.—He found hym in a deserte land, in a voyde grounde, and in a roarynge wildernesse.

Hosea 10. 11.—Ephraim was unto me as a cow that is used to go to plowe, therefore I loved him, and fell upon his neck. I drove Ephraim. Juda plowed, and Jacob played the husbondeman.

Edgar says that, whatever may be said of its accuracy as a translation, its intrinsic reasonableness strongly commends the following :—

Prov. 26. 4–5.—Give not the foole an answer *after* his foolishnesse, lest thou become like unto him; but make the foole an answer *to* his foolishnesse, lest he be wise in his own conceate.

Strikingly rendered also is Job 19. 20.—My bone hangeth to my skin, and the flesh is away ; only there is left me the skynne about my teeth.*

* *Bibles of England.*

The frontispiece is an emphatic recognition of the
share borne by the king in this work. It is divided
into four compartments. In the first the Almighty is
seen in the clouds with outstretched arms. Two scrolls
proceed out of His mouth, to the right and to the left.
On the former is the verse : " The word which goeth
forth from me shall not return to me empty, but shall
accomplish whatsoever I will have done." The other is
addressed to Henry, who is kneeling at a distance, bare-
headed, with his crown lying at his feet. The scroll
says : " I have found me a man after my own heart, who
shall fulfil all my will." Henry answers, " Thy word is a
lantern unto my feet." Immediately below, the king is
seated on his throne, holding in each hand a book, on
which is written " The Word of God." One of these he
is giving to Cranmer and another bishop,—who, with a
group of priests, are on the right of the picture,—saying,
" Take this and teach it." The other, on the opposite
side, he holds out to Cromwell and the lay peers, and the
words are, " I make a decree that, in all my kingdom, men
shall tremble and fear before the living God." A third
scroll, falling downward over his feet, says alike to peer
and prelate, " Judge righteous judgement ; turn not
away your ear from the prayer of a poor man." The
king's face is directed sternly towards the bishops, with
a somewhat threatening expression, as if to let the world
know who is to be Head of the Church now. In the
third compartment Cranmer and Cromwell are distribut-
ing the Bible to kneeling priests and laymen, and at the
bottom a preacher with a benevolent face is addressing a
crowd from a pulpit in the open air. He is commencing
a sermon from the text, " I exhort, therefore, that, first of
all, supplications, prayers, intercessions, and giving of
thanks be made for all men—for kings." At the word
kings the people are shouting " God save the King."
And at the extreme left, at a jail window, a prisoner is
joining in the cry of delight, as if he were being delivered
from bondage, like the Bible, long bound in an unknown
tongue. However, the work never cost Henry a penny.

Christopher Anderson tells us that he is said to have diced away the bells of suppressed houses, and lost thousands of the spoil at play, but he certainly never spent his money in printing Bibles.

This large title-page has been said to be the work of Hans Holbein the younger, though Wornum, in his *Life of Holbein*, pronounces against it. Mr. W. H. Carpenter, keeper of the engravings in the British Museum Library, however, gives his name, and it is certain that Henry was

HOLBEIN, BY HIMSELF.
IN SPENCER COLLECTION AT ALTHORP.

Holbein's patron at this time. The famous painter of " The Dance of Death," and many other well-known works, came to England the second time in 1532, and soon afterwards produced his masterpiece, " The Ambassadors," about which so much has been written by Ruskin. It was about this time he painted for the king the great family picture of Henry VII., with Elizabeth of York, and also that of Henry VIII., with Jane Seymour and children, and it seems likely that such a piece of work as this frontispiece would be put into the hands of a well-known artist.

The art of wood-cutting had certainly been rescued from its early monopoly by the playing-card makers, and in the hands of Albert Durer and others was soon to become a thing of beauty and a joy for ever. Our readers will agree, however, as they look at this great childish production that its hour had not yet come. Nothing is more comic than the early wood-cutting, especially that in the Dutch Bibles.*

The Great Bible has one special distinction. Its rendering of the Psalter is the one permanently used in the Church of England Prayer Book. When the "Bishops' Bible" succeeded this one, no attempt was made to substitute the new Psalter for this older one. And when the last Revision of the Prayer Book came, in 1662, the people had grown familiar with it, and though some pleaded for the Authorised Version, it retained its place. It was felt to be "smoother and more easy to sing," and Westcott analyses and defends this popular judgment, though the Authorised Version is almost always more correct. Certainly we cannot wonder that a great musician should prefer, "Why do the nations so furiously rage together!" So, whilst the Gospels and Epistles were directed to be taken from the Authorised Version more than two centuries ago, the Psalter was left unchanged. The present Prayer Book version of the Psalms, however, does not exactly correspond with any great Bible, and Psalm xxxviii. 10 has "sight" for "light."

The printing of the Great Bible was commenced in Paris, where the best materials were to be found, and the work was undertaken by Grafton and Whitchurch. Richard Grafton not only devoted himself to such work, but was an historian, his *Chronicle at large* having afterwards a considerable reputation. Both he and Whitchurch were excluded from the pardon in Queen Mary's proclamation at her Coronation in 1554.

They were afraid of being interrupted in their work, as Tyndale had been before them, and not without reason. In the middle of the winter of 1538, the Inquisition, caring

* *Origin of Wood Engraving*, Lewis, 1811.

neither for the countenance of the English ambassador, nor the express license of Francis, the King of France, both of which had been secured, issued an order against the printer, and summoned all parties engaged to appear. Francis Regnault was the printer employed, Grafton attending to business matters, but fortunately they had received notice of what was intended against them, and had sent a large portion of the sheets to England, whither they now followed them, leaving the remainder to their fate. A few were burned, but the rest were sold to a haberdasher "to lap his caps in," the officer in charge thinking he might as well make something for himself.

The ambassador at this time was the infamous Bonner, then Bishop of Hereford. The secret history of the whole affair is not yet written, but it would appear that he showed great interest in the undertaking, and forwarded it. He became very friendly with Grafton and Whitchurch, and still more with Coverdale. He insisted on their being frequently at his table, either at dinner or supper, and would often be found at the house of the printer. Certainly, when he afterwards became Bishop of London, he sent for Grafton, and made great promises of how he would promote the Word of God in his diocese. So this " Ecclesiastical Nero, the disgrace of the Church of England in the sixteenth century," as Dean Hook calls him, promised very different things at this time. He had a New Testament printed in English and Latin, and took a great many of them to give his friends. But his vile temper showed itself in these early " Protestant " days, and he so behaved himself in the presence of the Pope that the astonished and enraged Pontiff talked of throwing him into a cauldron of melted lead. He offended the French king, Francis I., also so hugely at this very time of his residence in Paris that his Majesty desired him to write three things to the king his master: that his ambassador was a great fool; that he (Francis) caused better justice to be done in his realm in a month than they did in England in a whole year; and that if it were not for the love he bore his master he should have an hundred strokes with a halbert.

By and by he took his revenge, when he whipped his Protestant prisoners with his own hands till he was tired with the violence of the exercise, and once tore out the beard of a weaver, and that he might give him a specimen of burning, held his hand to a candle till the sinews and veins shrunk and burst. Well may Dean Hook close his long account of him by saying, " Edmund Bonner, with his contemporary, Stephen Gardiner, have made Romanism so odious in the eyes of Englishmen that Romanisers have never since been able to maintain a permanent footing in our Church."

And yet he actually said to Grafton at this time :

" To tell you, Master Grafton, before God (for that was commonly his oath) the greatest fault that I ever found in Stokesley was for vexing and troubling of poor men, as Lobley, the bookbinder, and others for having the Scripture in English ; and, God willing, he did not so much hinder it, but I will as much further it ; and I will have of your Bibles set up in the Church of Paul's at the least in sundry places six of them ; and I will pay you honestly for them, and give you hearty thanks." Which words, says Foxe, who is constantly giving his authorities, he spoke in the hearing of divers credible persons, as Edmund Stile, Grocer, and others. But this was when he was willing to do anything to please Cromwell, against whom he said the strongest things when he had fallen.

CHAPTER XXI

THE COMPLETION OF THE GREAT BIBLE

"All's well that ends well."

AFTER a time, however, the printers stole back again and found that the Inquisition had not done its work so well as usual. They recovered the presses, type, and workmen, and eventually even the haberdasher's cap paper. Then, setting up again, the work was at length completed in April 1539, two parchment copies being printed for the king and Cromwell, and the remainder on paper. Cromwell's fine parchment copy is to be found in the library of St. John's College, Cambridge, but where the printing was finished is still doubtful. Some say in London, and that the wrath of man thus praised God, for the interference of the Inquisition thus introduced into England the materials and men best suited to carry out the translation. Some say in Flanders, and if so probably at Antwerp, and in any case there were seven distinct editions within three years, closely resembling one another. So, for the time, the "heretics, new-fangled fellows, English Biblers, Cobblers of Divinity, Fellows of the new Faith," as they complained that they were called, had completely triumphed.

The Bible was mostly allowed to speak for itself, some of the previous notes having given the chief offence. A few marginal notes were incorporated in the first impression, which, however, were afterwards omitted. The note on Matt. xvi. 18, for instance, is as follows :—

"That is," saith St. Austin, " upon the confession which

thou hast made, acknowledging me to be Christ, the Son of the living God, I build my Congregation or Church."

Now at length there was free course for the Word of the Lord, at least for a season. Every parish was to set a Bible up in its church, under a penalty of forty shillings a month, half the expense being borne by the minister and half by the people. A Royal Declaration was issued stating his Majesty's pleasure that his subjects should improve themselves in the knowledge of their duty to God and himself, and that the most likely way of attaining this end was to allow them the free use of the Bible in their mother tongue.

Hollinshead says that it was in September 1538 that Cromwell first sent out injunctions to all bishops and curates to have a Bible of the largest volume, and it was at the same time that all notable images to which pilgrimages were made, as those at Walsingham, Ipswich, and Worcester, were removed, as also shrines of "Counterfeit saints," like that of Thomas à Becket at Canterbury. Many of the images were brought up to London, and burnt at Chelsea by the Lord Privy Seal. No more could the parings of St. Edward's toe-nails be seen, nor the coals that roasted St. Lawrence. The girdle of the Virgin had been exhibited in eleven different places at the same time, but now it was to be found in none. At Hales, in Gloucester, the blood of Christ, brought from Jerusalem, had been shown for generations, but it only revealed itself to the absolved penitent. The phial had a thick and opaque side, and a transparent one. Into this the fresh blood of a duck was introduced every week, and the dark side only shown to rich pilgrims till they had freely expended their money, when the transparent side, showing the blood, was turned towards them, to their wonder.

Perhaps the most ingenious money-making contrivance was at Boxley in Kent, a miraculous crucifix called the Rood of Grace. The lips, eyes, and head of the image moved on the approach of its votaries, the eyes goggling, the lips hanging, the jaws shaking, according to the coin given. This was brought by Hilsey, the Bishop of

Rochester, to St. Paul's Cross, and there broken up in the presence of a great crowd, the wheels and springs by which it was moved being exposed.

Complaints have been made of the strong language used by Tyndale and others, but how could honest men speak with bated breath of these money-making impositions on the credulity of the people. They abounded, and were connected with the grossest cruelties against those who exposed them. The *North British Review* gives a list of those at Glasgow alone, from which we extract the following :—

" The priests of Glasgow appear to have been particularly favoured with choice articles of holiness. An inventory of them has been preserved. First, we have a bit of wood of the Cross; item, a golden vial, with part of the hair of the Blessed Virgin; item, a golden vial, containing part of the coat of St. Kentigern and Thomas Becket; item, in another golden casket, the mouth of St. Ninian ; item, part of the zone of the Blessed Virgin ; item, in a small vial of crystal, part of the milk of the B.V. ; item, a bit of the manger in which Christ lay ; item, in a small saffron-coloured vial, the oil which emanated from the tube of St. Kentigern ; item, another casket with the bones of St. Blasius and Eugenius; item, part of the comb of St. Catharine ; item, a small bag with part of the sweat of St. Martin ; item, a precious bag, with the breasts of St. Kentigern and Thomas Becket; item, four other sacks with the bones of saints; item, a wooden chest with many small relics ; and at last, when the person making the inventory was getting tired of his duty, he sums up the whole with—Item, two linen sacks full of the bones of Kentigern, Tenaw, and different other saints. Can there be a more wretched exhibition of human folly, or the picture of a more debasing superstition ! "

It was all this rubbish that had so fired the soul of Tyndale in Gloucestershire. " As sure as God is in Gloucester " meant that absurd forms and ridiculous ceremonies were a little more abundant there than elsewhere. The kissing of the thumb nails previous to engaging in prayer, the flinging of holy water at the devil, and the offering of a big cheese every year to St. White, went on before his eyes. Being an agricultural country, it was thought desirable to invoke the assistance of a special saint to protect the cream and cheese against the accidents of the weather, and the depredations of the fairies and the Welshmen. Though who St. White was is a mystery even to those versed in such lore. Perhaps she was a canonised dairymaid, or it may have been St. Witta, a German bishop of the eighth century, and a friend of Boniface.*

Burnet says that at Reading they had an angel's wing which brought over the spear's point that pierced our Saviour's side, and let no one imagine that this mass of absurdities simply attracted a few brainless people. At the Canterbury Jubilee it was thought 100,000 people were present. And when Henry VIII. put an end to all this imposture, instead of the authorities in Rome disowning it, he was compared to the worst princes that ever ruled, to Pharaoh, Belshazzar, Nero, Diocletian, and Julian—the latter more especially, as they called him an Apostate. The Pope put the kingdom under an interdict, and required all Christians to make war upon the king, and make slaves of his subjects.

It was the same abroad. At Wittenberg Luther might see a fragment of Noah's ark, some soot from the furnace of the Three Children, a piece of wood from the cradle at Bethlehem, some hair from the beard of St. Christopher, and thousands of other relics.

And remember that all this rubbish was supported by the highest authorities in the Popery of the time. For instance, the inducements to keep up the fame of "the holy blood of Hayles" are given at length by Hearne in the notes to Leland's *Collectanea*. Miracles were said to be wrought every day. Pope John XXIII. granted to the abbot for evermore power to have eleven confessors to forgive the pilgrims their sins. Pope Eugene IV. confirmed this and granted "seven yere and three lents" to

* Demaus, *Life of Tyndale*.

those who came down with their money.   Pope Calix III.
and fifteen cardinals also made great promises to those who
" put to their helping hands to the welfare of that foresaid
monastery at Hayles." *

The helping hands were put to such places so generously
that the wealth of the most famous of them became
fabulous.   Becket's shrine at Canterbury had a prodigious
number of precious stones, and a thousand pounds was
presented there in a single year, whilst the offerings at
Christ's altar were insignificant.   And this when the
common people were miserably poor, and perished by
thousands for the want of proper food, sanitation, and
medicine.

So down fell the monasteries in this reforming age, first
the small ones, and then the great.   In a play published
soon afterwards, Cromwell is made to answer Gardiner,
who is defending them :

> "I am no enemy to religion,
> But what is done it is for England's good.
> What did they serve for but to feed a sort
> Of lazy abbots and of full-fed Friars !
> They neither plough nor sow, and yet they reap
> The fat of all the land, and suck the poor." †

The suppression of the monasteries, however, was
begun by Wolsey, a cardinal of the Church, partly to
raise funds for his New College at Oxford.   Doubtless
they had become in many cases very corrupt, and the
destruction of the "black book" containing the Visitors'
charges, in Queen Mary's reign, is significant.   What
were they doing with all their money too, which Milton
calls the poison of the Church, the quinsy of truth ?   It is
difficult to see why a few clergy should need such large
sums to practise poverty.   At Abingdon there were only
25 in residence, and the revenues were £2000 a year ; at
Battle 17, and they had £1000 ; at St. Albans 37, with
£2000 ; at Bury 45, with £2000 ; all which figures

* *Acts and Monuments.*   Addenda to vol. v.
† *Lord Cromwell.*   A play by W. S., 1613.

must be multiplied by about 15 or 17 to represent present value.*

Of course both images and monasteries had their defenders, and at Shrewsbury, where an image had been removed, the following rhyme was circulated :—

> " The parson's the man !
> Let him do what he can.
> He'd for gain leave his God in the lurch.
> Could Iscariot do more,
> Had it lain in his power,
> Than turn the Lord out of the Church ? "

The vicar replied, however :

> " The God I adore
> Is mighty in power,
> The one only living and true.
> But that God of yours,
> That I turned out of doors,
> Had about as much power as you.

> But since you bemoan
> This God of your own.
> Cheer up, my disconsolate brother.
> Though it seem very odd,
> Yet if that be your God,
> Any duffer can make you another."

Bridgett attempts to show that the rood at Boxley was not used superstitiously, but he quotes Archbishop Warham saying that people came there from every part of the country.

* *T. Cromwell*, A. Galton.

CHAPTER XXII

CRANMER AND HIS BIBLE WORK—CROMWELL'S FALL

> " Step after step
> Through many voices crying right and left,
> Have I climbed back into the primal Church,
> And stand within the porch, and Christ with me."
> TENNYSON'S " Queen Mary."

> "O momentary grace of mortal men
> Which we more hunt for than the grace of God !
> Who builds his hopes in air of your fair looks
> Lives like a drunken sailor on a mast,
> Ready, with every nod, to tumble down
> Into the fatal bowels of the deep."
> SHAKESPEARE.

IN his exposition of the Sermon on the Mount, Tyndale spoke out about the absurdity of the monastic life, and the way it impoverished the country. He says on Matt. v. 20.

"God's law is pure and single, 'Love thy neighbour,' whether he be good or bad ; and by love God meaneth to help at need. Now when God biddeth thee to get thy living, and somewhat over to help him that cannot ; if thou, with thirty or forty others, get you to wilderness, and not only help not your neighbours, but also rob a great number of two or three thousand pounds yearly, how love ye your neighbours ? Such men help the world with prayer, thou wilt say to me. Thou wert better to say 'they rob the world with their hypocrisy.' For if I stick up to the middle in the mire, like to perish without present help, and thou stand by and wilt not succour me, but kneelest down and prayest, will God hear the prayers of such an hypocrite ? God biddeth thee so to love me

CRANMER, ARCHBISHOP OF CANTERBURY.

that thou put thyself in jeopardy to help me ; and that thine heart, while thy body laboureth, do pray and trust in God that he will assist thee, and through thee to save me. An hypocrite that will put neither body nor goods in peril for to help me at my need loveth me not, neither hath compassion on me ; and therefore his heart cannot pray, though he wag his lips ever so much."

Of course the Pope was highly indignant at the suppression of the monasteries, but their gross profligacy had been the subject of Papal admonitions only in 1490.

So it was Scripture against all that had been put in its place, and Cromwell's injunctions were not only for the Bibles being placed in the churches, but for encouragement being given to the people to read them :—" Item, that you shall discourage no man privily or apertly from the readyne or heryne of the sayde Bible, but shall expressely promote, stire, and exhorte every person to reade the same as that whiche is the very lively Worde of God ; that every Christen person is bounde to embrace, believe, and folowe, yf they loke to be saved ; admonysshyng them neverthe- lesse to avoyd all contention and altercation therein, but to use an honest Sobrietie in the inquisition of the trewe sense of the same, and to referre the explication of obscure places to men of higher judgement in Scripture."

In making such provision Cromwell was simply going back to the custom of the early Christian Churches, in which it was common to have a large Bible in some convenient place. Paulinus wrote on the wall of the Secretarium at Nola :

" Si quem sancta tenet meditandi in lege voluntas ;
    Hic poterit residens sacris intendere libris." *

Certainly a little more instruction was needed if Michael Ward can be trusted, who said about this time :—

* " If any one is piously disposed to meditate in God's law, here he may sit and employ himself in reading the holy books " (Bingham, *Antiquities*).

"Who is there can say even the Lord's Prayer in English! who can tell one article of his faith! who had once heard of any of the 10 Commandments! If we were sick of the pestilence, we ran to St. Rock; if of the ague, to St. Parnil or Master John Shorne. If men were in prison, they prayed to St. Leonard. If the Welshman would have a purse, he prayed to David Gathorne."*
But now the Churches had plenty of inquirers as well as listeners, and the doctrines, at last clearly read out, began to be in many places the common subject of conversation.

Cranmer appears to have had no direct connection with the Great Bible in its first edition ; but his followed in the spring of 1540, and then one edition succeeded another. What a name for raising a debate ! It is certain, however, that in days when good preaching was the rarest thing, Cranmer was a simple, earnest preacher of the main truths of the Bible. That, along with this, he was one of the greatest promoters of learning, and received in his palace at Lambeth such men as Bucer, who had made Strasburg a centre of Protestant light and learning, and eventually became Regius Professor of Divinity at Cambridge until his death. That he was also a liberal and generous-hearted man, and under special pressure, after the closing of the monasteries, fitted up one of his own manor houses as a hospital for soldiers who had returned from the wars on the Continent wounded, and were too often little cared for.

Mr. Fry says that in the whole of Cranmer's correspondence with Cromwell in 1538 there is not one allusion to the Bible. The Great Bible was emphatically Cromwell's work, and without his importation of types and men, Cranmer would not afterwards have been able to proceed as he did. When Cranmer followed him, however, in the same work, he brought out six editions, one after another, and there were probably 21,000 printed, though copies are now very rare and valuable. After most careful examination, Mr. Fry comes to the conclusion that many of the "made up" volumes were

* *Dialogue or Familiar Talk*, 1754.

CANTERBURY CATHEDRAL, THE MARTYRDOM TRANSEPT.
CRANMER PASSED FROM THIS TO BE A MARTYR HIMSELF.

first issued in that form.* The marginal notes were corrected, and there was a careful exclusion of everything relating to Tyndale, now burnt as a heretic.

What was especially new in these Cranmer Bibles was the Preface written by the archbishop himself, and doing him much honour. This was inserted in many of the editions, and he says to those who would shut up the the Bible:

" I marvel much that any man should be so mad as to refuse in darkness, light; in hunger, food; in cold, fire. For the Word of God is light—Thy word is a lantern to my feet. It is food—man shall not live by bread only, but by every word of God. It is fire—I am come to send fire on the earth, and what is my desire but that it be kindled. I would marvel at this, save that I consider how much custom and usage may do."

But he speaks with equal plainness to those who abused the Scripture, and all whose holiness consisted in talking. Quoting Gregory Nazianzen, he says: " The learning of a Christian man ought to begin of the fear of God, and end in matters of high speculation, and not contrarily to begin with high speculation and to end in fear." In fact, he says, there are two sorts of people, some being too slow and needing the spur ; and others too quick, and needing the bridle. In the former sort are all those that refuse to read the Scripture in the vulgar tongue; in the latter, those who by their inordinate reading, indiscreet speaking, contentious disputing, or licentious living, slander and hinder the Word of God. The whole Preface may be found in the Appendix to Strype's *Life of Cranmer*.

Anthony Marler, a citizen of London, of the Haberdashers' Company, bore all the expense of the folio editions printed in 1539–40, presenting a fine copy in vellum to Henry VIII., which is now in the British Museum. Anderson quotes the minutes of the Privy Council at Greenwich, 25th April, 33 of Henry VIII.—that is 1541:

" It was agreed that Anthony Marler, of London,

* *Great Bible*, F. Fry, F.S.A.

Merchant, might sell the Bibles of the Great Bible unbound for x shillings sterling, and bound, being trimmed
with bullyons for xii shillings sterling."

There was a good deal of backwardness in providing
such large and expensive Bibles, however, and we find
Marler representing himself to the Privy Council as a
ruined man, unless some further steps were taken to promote the sale of the Bibles he had printed, an order being
consequent upon this that the last day for the purchase
of the book was fixed for Hallow Masse." * On 12th
March 1542 a patent was granted him " to print the
Bible in English," a former prohibition having denied
that right to any except with Cromwell's license.†

It was at this very time of Bible opening and reading
that the " Bloody Bill " was passed, showing the need of
them in the clearest light. Its date was 7th June 1540,
and the Chancellor opened Parliament by saying that it was
his Majesty's earnest desire to extirpate from his kingdom
all diversities of opinion with regard to religion. Six
Articles were accordingly drawn up which asserted the
real presence in the Eucharist, the Communion in one
kind, the perpetual obligation of Vows of Chastity, the
utility of private Masses, Celibacy, and the utility of
Auricular Confession. All who did not subscribe to this
statute were to be burnt alive, beheaded, or stripped of their
property. It is to Cranmer's honour, who knew perfectly
well what it might mean to him in these difficult days,
that he opposed might and main the passing of this
measure. Henry ordered him at length to leave the
House. He refused to do so, saying that it was not man's
business but God's. The act was passed, however, like
everything else upon which Henry had set his mind, and
in a few months five hundred were thrown into prison.
" Those who are against the Pope," said a foreigner, " are
burned ; those who are for him are hanged." Latimer and
Shaxton, Bishops of Worcester and Salisbury, resigned their

---

* Nicolas, *Proceedings Privy Council*, vol. vii.
† This was dated November 14, 1539. See Rymer, *Acta Regia*.
Rapin III.

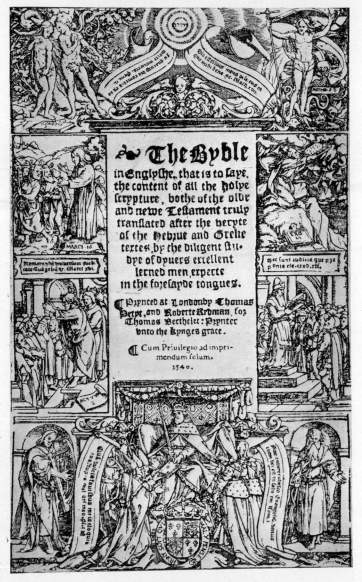

TITLE TO GREAT BIBLE, 1540.

sees, but as for Shaxton, on being pressed again to sign the Articles in 1534, and at last being condemned to be burnt to death, he made an abjuration to save his life.

Of course, Gardiner had a leading hand in this atrocious Act of the Six Articles, but Foxe says they might seem to have been written not with the ink of Stephen Gardiner, but with the blood of a dragon, or rather the claws of the devil. Scarcely might a man speak any word of Christ and His religion, but he was in peril of these Six Articles, so curious and subtle was their wording. Maitland thinks they were chiefly to frighten people,* and their severity was certainly so horrible that relaxation came before long, but not until some noble blood had been shed. There have been some fiendish things done in England, and we have given one or two examples of them where we might have given hundreds pertinent to our history. But perhaps the foulest of all was the judicial murder of Anne Askew, not long before this miserable reign closed. Though a little anticipating, we will give an account of this, as illustrating what took place under such Acts as these.

Anne Askew was the second daughter of Sir William Askew, of Kelsey, in Lincolnshire, and this lovely and noble victim was only about twenty-five years of age when she suffered the most horrible death on record. Her elder sister died, and she was compelled to marry against her will, and when very young, a wealthy neighbour, called Kyme, who was to have married her sister. For her love of the Bible and its truths, her husband drove her out of the house. She went to London, and soon became friendly with some of the principal ladies of the Court.

She was very brave and plain spoken, and was soon marked out for destruction by such Hell-hounds as Gardiner and Bonner. The account of her examinations occupies many pages in Foxe's *Acts and Monuments,* and was drawn up by herself, at the earnest request of her friends. Briefly, her confession of faith closes thus :

* *Essays on the Reformation.*

"Finally, I believe all those Scriptures to be true which Christ hath confirmed with His most precious blood. Yea, and St. Paul saith, those Scriptures are sufficient for our learning and salvation, that Christ hath left here with us ; so that I believe we need no unwritten verities to rule His Church with. But as concerning your Mass, as it is now used, I do say and believe it is the most abominable idol that is in the world ; for my God will not be eaten with teeth, neither yet dieth He again."

When she was condemned, she was let down into a dungeon at the Tower, where Sir Anthony Knevet, the Lieutenant, commanded his jailer to put her on the rack. The fiends wanted her to condemn some of the Court ladies, suspected of sharing Protestant views, such as Lady Herbert, the Queen's sister, and the Duchess of Suffolk. But nothing could be extracted from her, and she said she had lately lived by gifts from apprentices in the streets, which her maid went out and got for her. When Knevet thought things had gone far enough, and was about to take her off the rack, Wriothesley, the Chancellor,* commanded the Lieutenant to strain her on the rack again. He refused, and then Wriothesley and a creature called Rich, throwing off their gowns, racked her with their own hands. The consequence was that when the day of her execution came she was unable to walk, and was brought into Smithfield in a chair. When letters were brought to her, offering her pardon if she would recant, she would not look at them. The cowardly wretches who were in charge, Wriothesley, the old Duke of Norfolk, the Earl of Bedford, and the Lord Mayor, were afraid lest they should be injured by the gunpowder that was used, and it took a good deal of explanation to quiet their fears. But this lovely and constant lady had no fears, and died with three others, Shaxton the recanter being ordered to preach to them. Yes, the Apostate might preach, but such a piece of history will preach as long as

---

* This fiend was a renegade, being an "earnest doer against the Pope in my Lord Cromwell's time."—BALE.

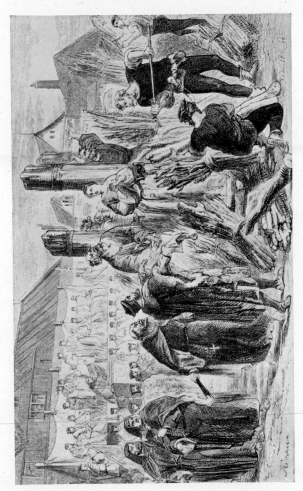

THE BURNING OF ANNE ASKEW AND OTHERS.

there are any men to see the difference between light and darkness, good and evil, sweet and bitter.*

The Commissioners who carried out the Six Articles matched them. In the Metropolis they were ignorant, headstrong, and bloodthirsty, "such as had read no part of Scripture in English, or in any wise favoured such as had, or loved the preachers of it." They sat in Mercer's Chapel, close by the Old Jewry, Cheapside, and over-stepping their commission they inquired who read the Bible in Church. The prisons could not contain all whom they brought to trial.

Of course there were martyrs of a Catholic type as well as Protestants, both in this reign and long before it. John Bale gives a list of them, and glories in the early ones of the Primitive Church here before such names as Catholic and Protestant were known, and when it acknow-ledged no authority of the Romish Pope. Such were Emerita, Amphibalus, Alban, Aaron, Julius, and Dinothus, who were as sheep among wolves. But "the Popish martyrdoms, compared to the martyrdoms of Anne Askew and her faithful company, are as a rusty iron to pure silver." England has had her true martyrs, however, for ages, he says, who have been "cruelly burnt if they did but read the Testament of God in their mother tongue; and their spiritual tyrants of Rome do not as yet repent them of that mischief, but continue therein."

We are not always able to agree with Gairdner in his recent volume, from which we have often quoted, but every one will agree with the way he closes his account of Anne Askew :

"How little is it understood, in any age, that the world is governed by spiritual influences and not by mere brute force! The burning of books was futile, for the burning of martyrs read a deeper lesson."

The Great Bible was the culminating point of a great struggle. The Right Honourable W. E. Gladstone said, in

* Bale draws out an elaborate parallel between Blandina, the famous second century martyr, and Anne Askew. It extends over two large pages. *Select Works of John Bale, D.D.*, Parker Society.

16

opening the Caxton Exhibition in 1877, that it was the climax and consummation of the art of printing up to that time. And Mr. Henry Stevens, F.S.A., adds that, considering the times and the state of the market; that as it was a wholly private, individual, and mercantile enterprise, carried on at great peril and risk by Marler, Grafton, Whitchurch, and other City merchants, in spite of ecclesiastical bigots not yet all dead,—it may be considered the greatest effort of the press even to the present day.* With seven distinct editions, 1539–41, of these great and magnificent volumes scattered throughout the land, 11,000 in the parish churches, and 20,000 in the families of the nobility and gentry, it was impossible for the nation not to advance.

Cromwell just lived to see his great project executed, and then fell, deserted by his king, whom he had often terrorised, but for whom he had done so much. Tudor absolutism was chiefly his creation, bearing fruit a century later in the execution of Charles I. His master should not have deserted him, but he had struck down More and Fisher, Courtenay and Pole, and his own turn came. *Tam aris quam aratris.* But just as Copernicus received his immortal book, on which his mind had been so long occupied, on his death-bed, so Cromwell lived to see his Bibles in every part of the land. Cranmer was the only man faithful to his friend. He wrote the king an eloquent letter in his defence, a very dangerous thing to do. But the king said, on reading it, "The traitor Lord never extended pity nor mercy to one of his victims, and he shall receive none from me." All were against him. The nobility envied him, being of low birth. Gardiner and the Catholics hated him for his suppression of the monasteries. He used to call the clergy the king's half-subjects, on account of their oaths to the Pope. The Reformers found he could not protect them, even from burning. And the people suffered from his avarice, and had long mistrusted him. Besides a subsidy of 4s. in the pound from the clergy, he had just forced on in the

* *Bibles in the Caxton Exhibition.*

Parliament another of one-tenth and four-fifteenths from the laity. Catherine Parr had recently given the king minute particulars of his tyranny, her own relative, George Throckmorton, being in the Tower; and Cromwell himself said that the vengeance of Heaven had overtaken him at last.*

But he was a loving and kind master to his servants, and provided for them nearly all beforehand. He remembered favours done him, and rewarded them generously. And if he had really been a traitor to the king, he would not have lamented his death so soon, and wished he had him back again. But there was never any dependence on Henry VIII. for two months together, except in the case of Cranmer, to whom he was always faithful, and whose life he saved more than once.

Foxe says it was the general rule for those who suffered as martyrs to have grace and fortitude which made them quite different from others. Often also they went to their doom with alacrity and cheerfulness, and it was so at last with Cromwell, though at first the prospect of death filled him with fear. But on the dread morning (July 28, 1540) he found Lord Hungerford, likewise going to his execution, very heavy and doleful, and exclaimed, "Be of good comfort, for if you repent and be heartily sorry for what you have done, there is mercy enough with the Lord. And though the breakfast we are going to be sharp, yet trusting to the Lord, we shall have a joyful dinner." So we must leave him in the great beyond, of which Faber says:

> "There is no place where earth's failings,
>   Have such kindly judgment given."

Better to die than live in such times! The House of Lords condemned to death without trial, examination, or evidence, the most powerful minister of the age, a man whom they had declared to be worthy of being the Vicar-General of the Universe only just before. The Commons objected a little, but the king put on his brow-beating air,

* *Men and Women of the Reformation*, S. H. Burke.

and they yielded. Never was there a more memorable case of being hoist with his own petard, for the Act under which he died was his own framing.

In the Great Bibles issued subsequent to July 1540, the date of Cromwell's death, the circle in the large frontispiece occupied by his coat of arms is left a blank. The fixed price of these numerous Bibles was 12s. bound, and 10s. unbound, being about £9 and £7, 10s. of our money. They were frequently sold for less, however, and Church records show this, as for instance at Ashburton there is the following entry:—"A.D. 1540. I Paid vs. iiid. for a new booke called a Bybyll. Paid viiid. for a chaine for fastenynge the said booke." *

* Rev. R. Lovett, M.A.

CHAPTER XXIII

TAVERNER, THE LAY-TRANSLATOR

"The Truth of God is as a rock assailed by waves; each in succession may seem to overwhelm it, but the force of each is in measure spent upon that which has preceded it, and modified by that which follows. Each wave may make wild havoc amongst the detached pebbles at its base, whilst the rock itself is unmoved and uninjured."

S. P. TREGELLES, LL.D.

In November 1540 there came out another edition of the Great Bible, with the name and sanction of that very Bishop Tunstall who had tried to stop the sale of Tyndale's version. It is never to be forgotten, indeed, in considering the history of these days, what a long night of Papist abuses had preceded them. So long had the Bible been shut against the people that conscientious men might think they were doing God service by opposing its free circulation. To a certain order of mind change is profanity. We are told that even as early as Augustine's day, a bishop having publicly read the new translation of Jonah by Jerome, the people hearing the word rendered Hedera, which they had been accustomed to hear Cucurbita, accused the bishop of falsifying the Scriptures. There was quite a tumult about it! But it is at least worth noting that conversions took place very rapidly when the king authorised the reading of the Scriptures. Many who had had serious scruples found answers to them, and here we find one of the great enemies of Tyndale, only a few years after his death, carrying on the work for which he had been martyred. He was now Bishop of Durham, and with him Heath, Bishop of Rochester, was associated. Tunstall seems to have been a fairly good man, for the times. Fuller says the Bishopric of Durham had halcyon

days under God and good Cuthbert Tunstall, a learned
man of sweet disposition, rather devout to follow his own
than cruel to persecute the consciences of others. Wood
calls him a very good Grecian and Hebrician, but it was
his name chiefly that was wanted, and his work was
probably of the slightest. Cromwell having fallen soon
after the publication of the Great Bible, the sanction of
two eminent bishops was desirable for after editions.
All the better if they belonged to the party which had
opposed Cromwell, so as to show that this was not a
matter of parties. So on the title-page of the edition
which came out the very year that Cromwell was executed,
Tunstall and Heath are said to have "overseen and
perused" the translation, "at the commandment of the
King's Highness." Cranmer's Prologue is inserted, but
the Preface to the Apocrypha is left out. Afterwards,
when the tide turned, the two bishops disclaimed all
responsibility, so that probably they did scarcely anything,
and were unwilling to do that.

Tunstall had gone to Italy in his early days, and
absorbed some of the spirit of the Renascence in its home.
He studied at Padua, and was engaged in the diplomatic
service of Henry VIII., receiving ecclesiastical preferment
for his services,—quite a common thing. He was Wolsey's
agent at the famous Diet of Worms, and wrote to his
master that he believed there were a hundred thousand
Germans ready to lay down their lives in Luther's defence.*

It is a somewhat striking indication of the revival of
letters to find a layman bringing out a translation of his
own about the same time. This was Richard Taverner,
to whose work Westcott says that justice has scarcely
been done. He certainly presents a picturesque figure in
more ways than one. He was born at North Elmham in
Norfolk, educated at Benet College, Cambridge, and Christ
Church, Oxford, and at the latter became known as a reader
of Tyndale's New Testament when first they arrived at
Oxford. He was one of those imprisoned for a time
in the College cellar, in consequence, amongst the salt fish.

* *Cambridge History of Literature.*

A public Act of penance followed, such books being thrown
into a fire at Carfax, in the centre of the city. Later on
he was at the Inner Temple, and came under the patron-
age of Cromwell, being made a Clerk of the Signet in
ordinary. In Edward VI.'s reign, preachers being very
scarce, he received a licence as an Evangelist, and preached
in different churches throughout the kingdom. He wore
a velvet bonnet and a damask gown, with a gold chain
about his neck, and exercised his gifts as a lay preacher
both at Court and before his University. During Queen
Mary's reign he retired to his house at Norbiton Hill, and
remained there unmolested until the accession of Elizabeth.
He then presented her with a congratulatory epistle, and
was offered the honour of knighthood, which, however, he
refused. But he accepted later on the office of High Sheriff
of Oxfordshire, which he held for six years. He continued
to preach. He preached before the University in 1569,
wearing a sword at his side, and commencing:—
"Arriving at the Mount of St. Mary's, in the stony
stage (a pulpit of stone), where I now stand, I have
brought you some fine biscuits baked in the oven of
charity, and carefully conserved for the chickens of the
Church, the sparrows of the Spirit, and the sweet swallows
of salvation." Perhaps the man's pleasant humour
lengthened his life, in spite of his having been once
thrown into the Tower, as well as amongst the salt fish
in the cellar of his College, for he lived to be a very old
man. Henry VIII. made him a number of presents, and in
1545 he was returned to Parliament for Liverpool. His
preaching was of course unusual, but he had a special
licence for it. Other laymen have done the same, being
University men, such as Holcot. Sir T. More read lectures
on Augustine's *City of God*, in the Church of St. Lawrence,
Old Jewry, for some time after he was called to the Bar
at Lincoln's Inn. The University of Oxford possesses the
power of licensing, under sufficient safeguard.*
Taverner's Bible is something between a revision of
Matthew's and a new version. It was printed by John

* *Notes and Queries.*

Byddell in 1539, and was published under Royal authority. Some skill in Greek is shown, but in the dedication to the king, Taverner says that it is a work of such great difficulty that he found it could scarce be done by one or two persons, but rather required "both a deeper conferring of many learned wits together, and also a juster time and longer leisure." There is a table of principal matters, as in Matthew's Bible, and the Apocrypha is included. On the title-page is the somewhat singular expression—"Recognised by Richard Taverner." He affirms in the dedication that the king never did anything more acceptable to God and profitable to the advancement of true Christianity than when he sent forth the Bible in English, "though it would want another Cicero or Demosthenes to set forth what he had done for the Christian religion." This was the kind of thing that made Henry like a spoilt child.

Taverner was a lawyer, but there is no prolixity about his version, which aims at compression and vividness. The word "mercystock" is coined for Tyndale's roundabout "He it is that obtaineth grace for our sins." His regard for the Greek article led him to better renderings, such as "that was *the* true light," "I am *a* voice of one crying." It had been his humour sometimes to quote the law in Greek, and possibly this incited the printer to suggest such a work to him, which may be the origin of the version.

There are several pieces of independent translation in the Old Testament, and this Bible has an additional book at the end of the Apocrypha, viz. the Third Book of Maccabees, consisting of seven chapters. Westcott says that he has observed no help that he had for the Old Testament, except the Vulgate, but scarcely a page fails to show changes which are made for the sake of clearness and force. Thus "the child of death" becomes "worthy of death" (2 Sam. xii. 5); "of mine own mind" is altered to "of mine own head"; "a curtesye bawlme" is changed into "a quantity of bawlme."

A large proportion of Rogers's notes are absent, and

some are softened.   Thus, in the Table of principal matters, where Matthew begins " An altar was never commanded to be made but only to God," Taverner reads, " An altar was commanded to be made to God."   The section speaking of those that believe in Purgatory thus despising the passion of Christ, he omits altogether.

There were two editions, folio and quarto, and both the entire Bible and the New Testament were printed the same year.   The quarto edition was published in part, so that all might be able to secure a portion.   It was probably the first work to be ever so brought out.   The appearance of the Great Bible checked the sale, but both Bible and New Testament were reprinted, and the Old Testament was adopted in a Bible of 1551.

Cromwell no doubt favoured this Bible of Taverner's, but its influence on subsequent versions was not great. Some more translations came from the same pen, showing the layman's learning, amongst them being " The Confession of Faith of the Germans, with the Apology of Melanchthon."

He published also some " Postils," or Expositions of the Gospels and Epistles.   They did not receive any such sanction as to be entitled to rank with the Homilies, Foxe's *Acts and Monuments*, the Paraphrase of Erasmus, or the *Apology* of Bishop Jewel, all of which came to have some authority in the Church of England.   But two of them were adopted by Archbishop Parker, and published by authority of Queen Elizabeth, in her second Book of Homilies.   Twenty-two years had elapsed since they were issued, and " times of shaking" both in doctrine and discipline had been experienced such as are rarely known, and yet they were adopted without any alterations of importance, though they were on two of the most important services of the Church.

Taverner's Bible is seldom found complete.   The copy in Earl Spencer's Library, lent to the Caxton Exhibition, wants folios 55 to 60 in the New Testament, and H. Stevens says this hiatus was probably intended to be filled with a prologue to the Epistle to the Romans.

Here are two renderings from Judges, for which I am indebted to Lord Peckover.

5. 15.—Even so was Isakar sent to the valeye a fote, and put his life in a venture.

5. 27.—Betwene her feet he sprawled and laye deed lyke a wretche.

Taverner was employed by the printers, but says that it was only notable faults that he was desired to amend, and that it is absurd to suppose that a faultless translation could be made in a year's time by any single man. As further specimens of his work, we give:

Matt. 26. 30.—When they had given praises.

Luke 12. 29.—Be not carried in the clouds.

Edgar says that Taverner's adherence to the English text of Tyndale is much more noticeable and sometimes stranger than his occasional departures from it. Both render 1 Tim vi. 17, "Charge them that are ryche in this world that they be not exceedyng wyse."

CHAPTER XXIV

THE REACTION AND ITS CAUSES

"Systems, schemes, and hypotheses, all bred in the warm region of controversy, will, like meteors in a troubled sky, all have their turn to blaze and pass away. But the Bible is eternal, like the sun, the never failing source of life and light."

WARBURTON, *Divine Legation.*

So the new art of printing became a mighty force on the side of truth. Foxe exults in it, exclaiming—

"Hereby tongues are known, knowledge groweth, judgment increaseth, books are dispersed, the Scripture is seen, the Doctors be read, stories be opened, times compared, truth promoted, falsehood detected, and with finger pointed, and all through the benefit of printing."

But some time before Henry's death a reaction set in. The times were gathering a greater degree of hazard and perplexity. By declining to enter into a common Confession of Faith, Henry had estranged from him the Protestant princes of Germany. The Roman Catholic Powers had begun to form alliances against him. The Pope had held a Bull of Excommunication suspended over him, and some of the Reformers had assumed a license inconsistent with the king's views of supreme authority, and with the tranquillity of the realm. The arrest and almost immediate execution of such a man as Cromwell also was a terrible blow to the Reformers, and one of Henry's foulest crimes.

In 1542 it was proposed in Convocation that the New Testament should be still further revised, and that certain "majestic words" in the Latin copy should be transferred into this new version. The motion was made by Gardiner, and the words he wished to retain were exactly a hundred, and occupy seventeen lines in Collier's *History*. It was during the sixth session of a select Joint-Committee of both Houses of Convocation appointed to examine and amend the Great Bible that the proposition was made. Two sittings followed this, and then Henry sent to say that the two Universities had better be consulted. All dissented from this, except Cranmer and two others, the argument being that the Universities were "much sunk from their former considerableness," and that the learning of the nation lay mostly in Convocation. Cranmer, however, said he would stick by his master's will and pleasure, and the whole matter was allowed to drop.

The next year, only four years after the royal sanction, a Bill was passed prohibiting the use of Tyndale's translation altogether, and denying the Bible to all except the highest in the land. Neither in public nor private was any one belonging to the class of artificers, journeymen, servants, husbandmen, and labourers allowed to read any portion of God's Word. Thus did the tide turn directly after it had risen to its height, Burnet saying that what Henry did after this was by starts backwards or forwards as the humour took him.

There were two Acts, and by this one in 1543, Lords, Gentlemen, and Merchants might possess an English Bible, and some other religious books for the instruction of their families. But Cranmer himself seems to have been a favourer of this Bill, which denied it to all others, the preamble speaking of "many seditious and ignorant people," who abused the privilege granted to them. The stronger prohibition was in 1546, and not only were Tyndale's and Coverdale's Bibles forbidden, but any books set forth in the names of Tyndale, Frith, Joy, Bale, Barnes, Coverdale, Turner, Tracy, and all Protestant books in general. This latter Act was at Gardiner's suggestion and Wriothesley's, and Henry of course quite turned his back on his former opinions in sanction-ing it.*

Once Cranmer and Gardiner had a dispute in his presence on the giving of the Word of God to the people, Henry listening for some time attentively. Perceiving, however, the superiority of Cranmer's arguments in favour of it, the debate was suddenly broken up by Henry's exclaim-ing to Gardiner that such a novice as he was not fit to contend with an old experienced general.†

What results, then, had followed the opening of God's Word so disastrous that it was necessary to close it again? The preamble already referred to says that great diversity of opinion, animosities, tumults, and schisms had been occasioned by perverting the sense of the Scriptures. But what good thing has ever been without its abuses? and surely some might have been reckoned upon at first. If food in good quantity is set before a number of famished men, there will be the possibility of some injury, but that is better than starving. It is exactly what happened at the first publication of the Gospel, and is deplored by the Apostle: "Some things hard to be understood, which they that are unlearned and unstable wrest, as they do also other Scriptures unto their own destruction." But what conclusion does he draw? Not that the Scriptures are therefore to be put aside, but only that we are to beware lest we be led away with the error of the wicked, and fall from our own steadfastness. And as for the learning supposed to be necessary before the Word of God comes into the hands of the people, let Du Moulin speak: "Must one be skilled in Greek or Hebrew? But the Popes themselves, who give these rules, are often unskilful. ‡ And a knowledge of Hebrew cannot be attained but by the reading of the Old Testament. Must one have the learning which comes of studying the old Poets, with their lust

* The kingdom was also to be purged of all religious plays, inter-ludes, rhymes, ballads, and songs, which were said to be equally pes-tiferous and noisome to the peace of the Church.

† Rapin.

‡ Innocent III. derives the word " pascha "from the Passion. Another said that Cephas signifies a "head."

and war ?   Must one be abreast of philosophy ?   But the Apostles were not by any means; and some philosophers have been bitter enemies to the Christian religion.   Is not Scripture rather to be read to get learning ? "

The Bill became an Act, however, and soon Gardiner is found figuring in the renewed history of persecution. We have mentioned the Windsor martyrs, who were tried before a packed jury of College tenants, the Papists there not being numerous enough.   The description of their steadfastness unto death, right under Windsor Castle, so affected Henry that, for a while, the hands of the persecutors were stayed.   This was the way he got reported abroad, however; Richard Hilles. writing to Henry Bullinger at this time, says:

" The king has within these two months, as I wrote to John Burcher, burnt three godly men in one day.   For he has married the widow of a certain nobleman (Catherine Parr), and he is always wont to celebrate his nuptials by some wickedness of this kind." *

To the same period belongs the remarkable incident connected with the name of Patrick Hamilton.   He was nephew to the Regent in Scotland, and was arraigned under the ordinary charges urged against Protestants.   He had been betrayed by a Dominican friar, called Campbell, whom he had taken some pains to convince, and who insulted him at the stake.   He called him to answer at the judgment seat of Christ, and appealed to him whether he were not persuaded of the very truths for which he was persecuting him.   The friar went mad, fell into a fever, and died.

Certainly it must be admitted that some of the effects of the circulation of God's Word were bad.   Foolish people talked all the more foolishly, and hot reasoners got very warm on some Biblical subjects.   Many had not learnt what Augustine says, that Scripture is a large and high place, but the door is very low, so that the high and arrogant man cannot run in; or, to use the figure of Cheney, Bishop of Gloucester:

* *Original Letters*, Parker Society.

"In reading the Scriptures be you like the snail, for when he feels a hard thing against his horns, he pulls them in again. So when you come to hard matters of controversy, pull in your horns."

Sects professing the strangest doctrines sprang up, and became even dangerous to the State. There were Anabaptists, who held that every man was guided by the direct inspiration of the Holy Ghost, and that there was no need of any judge, magistrate, minister, or even of civil law; Antinomians, who persuaded themselves that they thought that all things were free to the saints, and amongst whom were to be found some of the vilest characters; members of the "Family of Love," and Davidians, called after David George, their leader, who announced himself to be the Messiah, denied the existence of either heaven or hell, and laughed at all kinds of self-denial. He promised that after death he would rise again at the end of three years; which he did, for the magistrate of the city where he was buried, when the time arrived, had him dug up and burnt, together with his writings, by the common hangman. Then there were Arians, Libertines, and Unitarians, and arguments on the most sacred subjects were conducted with such venom, that Hudibras cries out:

> "As if religion were intended
> For nothing else but to be mended,
> A sect whose chief devotion lies
> In odd, perverse antipathies;
> In falling out with that or this,
> And finding somewhat still amiss;
> More peevish, cross, and splenetic
> Than dog distract, or monkey sick."

But this was to be almost reckoned on for a time, and was not to be measured at all by the side of the incalculable benefits conferred on the nation by giving it the holiest body of truth which the world contains. Knowledge and religion had been separated, and if those that made the chasm would not build the bridge, let them not criticise the ruder workmanship of those who sought to "unite the pair so long disjoined, knowledge and vital piety." Coleridge has said :

"Those who examine a system by identifying it with its abuses and imperfections degrade their understandings, and are sure to prescribe remedies more dangerous than the disease." *

It is also to be remembered that a large proportion of the scandals which abounded at this period are to be attributed not to the circulation of the Scriptures, but to the suppression of the monasteries. Many who had been thrown out of them found it hard to support a livelihood, and the means which they adopted were often not such as established their character. One priest, in Derbyshire, had a church and an alehouse under the same roof, and kept them both going himself, there being a hole in the wall so that beer could be passed from the one to the other.

The suppression of the monasteries could not but make a vast difference in every way. The number was enormous. There were suppressed at different times in this one reign 645 monasteries, 90 colleges, 2374 chantries and free chapels, and 110 hospitals, the revenue of the whole amounting to £161,000, whilst the movables were worth half a million. Henry did not begin the work, and in 1513 had written to Leo x., eulogising the Religious Orders in England, Franciscans and Grey Friars being specially commended. He described them then as being "remarkable for Christian poverty, sincerity, charity, and devotion," however much he changed his mind afterwards.†

Wolsey really led the way in 1524, seizing on no fewer than forty small monasteries, in order to found his two colleges, and turning their inhabitants out of house and home. This was when he was a cardinal of the Romish Church, and Pope Clement vii. sanctioned what he did. Henry v. also suppressed a hundred monasteries in 1414, wanting money to carry on his war with France, and

* Lay sermon to the higher and middle classes.
† Ellis's *Original Letters*.

Henry VI. endowed Eton and King's College (Cambridge) with revenues which came from the suppression of alien priories.

To his honour be it said that Gardiner did not receive the smallest portion of the plunder, though he could often enough be a pliant tool of Henry's. The waste was fearful. Bale tells us that some monastic libraries were used to clean candlesticks; some to rub boots; some were sold to grocers and soap boilers; and large quantities were sent over the seas—whole shipfuls, to the great wonder of foreign nations. " I know a man," he says, " who bought the contents of two noble libraries for forty shillings, a shame be it spoken. He used the said books for ten years instead of grey (brown) paper, and yet he had sufficient for many years to come." The monasteries had employed about 200,000 men, women, and children, and often their new masters were not half so good to them. Churches were turned into shelters for sheep. The number of idle and sick poor became terrible, as well as worse offenders, and to meet the case there was an amended code of whipping, ear cutting, and pinching; and an improved specimen of the pillory, invented by Cromwell's brother. Stripping naked and whipping till the blood came was an everyday thing. Highwaymen were hanged on the nearest tree, and hanging, drawing, and quartering were dismally frequent.

Certainly a good deal was credited to the opening of the Bible, which had very little more connection with it than Tenterden Church steeple had with Goodwin Sands. Calvin has to defend Luther in the same way, and after speaking of Anabaptists and others who were no disciples of his, he says :

" The Reformers are no more bound to bear the odium of their impiety than Paul was to bear that of Hermogenes and Philetus. We must not be frightened out of good things because of a few abuses which the common sense of men will presently rectify."

Most likely a good many lies were told about the evil doings in the monasteries, but it is significant that the

17

" black book " containing the record is said to have been destroyed in Queen Mary's reign. And no one need pore over the " Comperta " preserved in the Record Office, for the Bishops' Registers are above suspicion, and substantiate some of the worst accusations. The facts about St. Rhadegund's Nunnery at Cambridge, suppressed as early as 1497 by the Bishop of Ely, and about St. Albans, are indisputable, if not illustrative, for those who wish to examine more fully an unpleasant subject. Creighton says, in his *Historical Essays*:

" The monks, as a body, were above the ordinary standard of morality, but they were not so far above it as to be a moral force in the community. They were lazy, ignorant, self-indulgent, and a hindrance to economic progress and ecclesiastical reform."

And probably their charities have been exaggerated. The houses were mostly apart from the centres of population, and their annals show but few traces of any thoughtful gifts.* Often this was not their fault, but it took twenty-six carts to convey away the treasures from Becket's shrine.

No doubt the spoil should have been put to better use. Most of the enormous sums made by the Dissolution went into the hands of the nobility and gentry. By purchase at very easy rates, or direct gifts from the Crown, they were made the fast friends of the new order of things. It was wrong, but most would agree with Hallam's summing up:

" However illaudable in its motive, this has proved, on the whole, more beneficial to England than any other disposition would have turned out."

Certainly the country was not really impoverished by what happened. It was poor enough before, in the days when monasteries abounded. At the very time when Tyndale published his first New Testament, some rebels in Norfolk said to the Duke, " My Lord, since you ask who is our captain, forsooth his name is Poverty, for he and his cousin Necessity hath brought us to this doing."

* *Reformation in England*, G. G. Perry, M.A.

CHAPTER XXV

FOXE'S "MERRY AND PLEASANT NARRATIVE"

"A little nonsense now and then
Is relished by the best of men."
SHAKESPEARE.

OH the horrors of this reign! Alas for the rarity of Christian charity! We might fill whole chapters with the persecutions of innocent people. Here, to open Foxe at random, is some of the bloody work of Longland, Bishop of Lincoln, who was one of the worst of the persecuting brood, in 1541.

"About the same time John Longland, Bishop of Lincoln, burned two upon one day, the one named Thomas Bernard, and the other James Morton; the one for teaching the Lord's Prayer in English, and the other for keeping the Epistle of St. James translated into English."

It would be only too easy to multiply such quotations. Some recanted, and a great stir was made the same year about the recantation of "Master Barber," an Oxford Master of Arts. Another who recanted was "Master Malary," a Cambridge Master of Arts, Scholar of Christ's College, who was sent to Oxford, to teach the Bible lovers there a lesson. He was to openly recant and bear his faggot, and listen to a sermon for the good of his soul, exhorting him to stop reading the Scriptures which Christ had commanded to be searched. But the whole narration is so illustrative of the temper and spirit of the two parties that were dividing the Church, so apropos to the subject, and so highly amusing, that, though it is a little long, we feel tempted to extricate it from Foxe's great volumes, and give it in his own words.*

* *Acts and Monuments*, vol. v.

A Merry and Pleasant Narration.

The time and place were appointed, that Master Malary should be brought solemnly into St. Mary's Church (the University Church), Oxford, upon a Sunday ; where a great number of the head doctors and divines, and others of the University were together assembled, besides a great multitude of citizens and town dwellers, who came to behold the sight. Furthermore, because that solemnity should not pass without some effectual sermon for the holding up of the Mother Church of Rome, Dr. Smith, reader then of the Divinity Lecture, was appointed to make the sermon at this recantation. Briefly, at the preaching of this sermon there was assembled a mighty audience of all sorts and degrees, as well of students as others. Few almost were absent who loved to see or hear any news ; insomuch that there was no place almost in the whole church which was not fully replenished with concourse and throng of people.

All things being thus prepared, cometh forth poor Malary, with his faggot upon his shoulder. Not long after, also, proceedeth the Doctor into the pulpit, to make his sermon, the argument whereof was wholly on the Sacrament ; the which Doctor, for the more confirmation of his words, had provided the Holy Catholic Cake, there to hang by a string before him in the pulpit. Thus the Doctor, with his God Almighty, entering his sermon, had scarce proceeded into the midst thereof, the people giving great silence with all reverence unto his doctrine, but suddenly was heard into the church, the voice of one crying in the street, " Fire, Fire ! " The party who thus cried in the street was called Henster, and the occasion of this exclamation came by a chimney that was on fire in the town.

This sound of fire being heard in the church, first of them that stood outermost next to the church door, so increased and went from one to another, that at length it came to the ears of the Doctors, and at last to the preacher himself, who, as soon as they heard the matter, being amazed with sudden fear, and marvelling what the matter should mean, began to look up into the top of the church, and to behold the walls. The residue, seeing them look up, looked up also. Then began they, in the midst of the audience to cry out with a loud voice, "Fire, Fire!" "Where?" saith one; "Where?" saith another. "In the church," saith one. The mention of the church was scarcely pronounced, when, as in one moment, there was a common cry amongst them, "The church is set on fire by heretics." And albeit no man did see any fire at all, yet, forasmuch as all men cried out so, every man thought it true that they heard. Then was there such fear, concourse, and tumult of people, through the whole church that it cannot be declared in words as it was in deed.

And as in a great fire, where fire is indeed, we see many times how one little spark giveth matter of a mighty flame, setting whole stacks and piles a-burning, so here, upon a small occasion of one man's word, kindled first a general cry, then a strong opinion, running in every man's head within the church, thinking the church to be on fire where no fire was at all. Thus it pleased Almighty God to delude these deluders; that is, that these great Doctors and wise men of the Schools, who think themselves so wise in God's matters as though they could not err, should see, by their own senses and judgments, how blinded and infatuated they were in these so small matters and sensible trifles.

Thus the strong imagination of fire being fixed in their heads, as nothing could remove them to think contrary but that the church was on fire, so everything that they saw or heard increased this suspicion in them, to make it seem most true, which was indeed most false. The first occasion that augmented this suspicion was the heretic there bearing his faggot, which gave them to imagine that all other heretics had conspired with him to set the church on fire.

After this, through the rage of the people, and running to and fro, the dust was so raised, that it showed as it had been the smoke of fire ; which thing, together with the outcry of the people, made all men so afraid, that, leaving the sermon, they began all together to run away. But such was the press of the multitude, running in heaps together, that the more they laboured, the less they could get out. For while they ran all headlong to the doors, every man striving to get out first, they thrust one another in such sort, and stuck so fast, that neither they that were without could get into the church again, neither they that were within could get out by any means. So then, one door being stopped, they ran to another little wicket on the north side, toward the College called Brasennose, thinking so to pass out. But there again was the like or greater throng. So the people, clustering, and thronging together, it put many in danger, and brought many to their end, by bruising of their bones or sides. Some yet are alive whose mother's arms were there broken. There was yet another door towards the west, which, albeit it was shut and seldom opened, yet now ran they to it with such sway that the great bar of iron, which is incredible to be spoken, being pulled out and broken by force of men's hands, the door, notwithstanding, could not be opened for the press or multitude of people.

At last, when they were there also past all hope to get out, then they were all exceedingly amazed, and ran up and down, crying out upon the heretics who had conspired their death. The more they ran about and cried out, the more smoke and dust rose in the church, even as though all things had now been on a flaming fire. I think there was never such a tumultuous hurly-burly rising so of nothing at all, nor so great a fear where there was no cause for fear, nor peril at all; so that if Democritus, the merry philosopher, sitting in the top of the church, and seeing all things in such safety as they were, had looked down upon the multitude, and beholden so great a number, some howling and weeping, running up and down, and playing the madmen, now hither, now thither, as being tossed to and fro with waves or tempests, trembling and

HIGH STREET, OXFORD.

quaking, raging and faring, without any manifest cause; especially if he had seen those great rabbins, the doctors, laden with so many badges or cognisances of wisdom, so foolishly and ridiculously seeking holes and corners to hide themselves in; gasping and sweating, and for very horror being almost beside themselves; I think he would have satisfied himself with this one laughter for all his lifetime; whilst one said that he plainly heard the noise of the fire, another affirmed that he saw it, and another swore that he felt the molten lead dropping down upon his head and shoulders. Such is the force of imagination when it is once grafted in men's hearts through fear. In all the whole company there was none that behaved himself more modestly than the heretic that was there to do penance; who, casting his faggot off from his shoulders upon a monk's head that stood by, kept himself quiet.

All the others, being careful for themselves, never made an end of running up and down and crying out. None cried out more earnestly than the Doctor that preached, Doctor Smith, who, in manner first of all, cried out in the pulpit, saying, "These are the trains and subtleties of the heretics against me. Lord, have mercy upon me; Lord, have mercy upon me." But might not God, as it had been, to speak with Job, out of a whirlwind, have answered again unto this preacher thus, "Thou dost now implore My mercy, but thou thyself showest no mercy, unto thy fellows and brethren. How doth thy flesh tremble now at the mention of fire! But you think it a sport to burn other simple innocents, neither do ye anything at all regard it. If burning and to suffer a torment of fire seem so grievous a matter unto you, then you should also have the like consideration in other men's perils and dangers, when you do burn your fellows and brethren! Or, if you think it but a light and trifling matter in them, go to now, do you also, with like courage contemn, and with like patience suffer now, the same torments yourselves. And if so be I should now suffer you, with the whole church, to be burned to ashes, what other thing should I do unto you, than you do daily unto your fellows and brethren.

Wherefore, since you so little esteem the death of others, be now content that other men should also little regard the death of you." With this, I say, or with some other like answer, if that either God, or human charity, or the common sense of nature would expostulate with them; yea, if there had been a fire indeed, who would have doubted but that it had happened unto them according to their deserts ? But now, worthy it is the noting, how the vain fear and folly of those Catholics either were deluded, or how their cruelty was reproved, whereby they, being better taught by their own example, might hereafter learn what it is to put other poor men to the fire, which they themselves here so much abhorred.

But to return again to the history of this pageant, wherein there was no danger at all, yet were they all in such fear as if present death had been over their heads. For almost all the churches in England are covered with lead, as in Germany they are for the most part tiled. In all this great maze and garboil, there was nothing more feared than the melting of the lead, which many affirmed that they felt dropping upon their bodies. Now in this sudden terror and fear, which took from them all reason and counsel, to behold what practices and sundry shifts every man made for himself, it would make not only Democritus and Heraclitus also to laugh, but rather a horse well near to break his halter. And none used themselves more ridiculously than such as seemed the greatest wise men, saving that in one or two peradventure somewhat more quietness of mind appeared. The younger and stronger of these ran up and down through the press, marvelling at the incivility of men, and waxed angry with the unmannerly multitude that would give no room to the doctors, bachelors, masters, and other graduates and regent-masters. But, as the terror and fear was common unto all men, so was there no difference made of persons or degrees, every man scrambling for himself. The violet cap, or purple gown, did there nothing avail the doctor; neither the master's hood, nor the monk's cowl, was there respected.

ST. MARY'S, OXFORD.

Yea, if the King or Queen had been there at that present, and in that perplexity, they had been no better than common people. After they had long striven and assayed all manner of ways, and saw no remedy, neither by force nor authority to prevail, they fell to entreaty and offering of rewards; one offereth twenty pound of good money, another his scarlet gown, so that any man would pull him out, though it were by the ears!

Some stood close under the pillars, thinking themselves safe, under the vautes of stone from the dropping of the lead; other some, being without money, and unprovided of all shift, knew not which way to turn them. One, being a president of a certain College, whose name I need not here utter, pulling a board out from the pews, covered his head and shoulders therewith against the scalding lead, which they feared much more than the fall of the church. How great a laughter would this also have ministered to Democritus to behold a certain grand paunch, who, seeing the doors stopped and every way closed up, thought by another compendious means to get out through a glass window, if it might be by any shift! But here the iron grates letted him; notwithstanding his greedy mind would needs attempt. When he had broken the glass, and was come to the space between the grates where he should creep out, first he thrust in his head with one shoulder, and it went through well enough. Then he laboured to get the other shoulder after; but there was great labour about that, and long he stuck by the shoulders, but at the last he got it through with much ado; for what doth not importune labour overcome! Thus far forth he was now gotten; but by what part of his body he did stick fast, I am not certain, neither may I feign, forasmuch as there be yet witnesses which did see these things, which would correct me, if I should do so. Notwithstanding, this is most certain, that he did stick fast between the grates, and could neither get out nor in. Thus this good man, being indeed a monk, and having but short hose, by the which way he supposed soonest to escape, by the same he fell into further inconvenience, making of one danger two. For, if the fire or lead had fallen on the outside, those parts which did hang out of the window had been in danger; and contrariwise, if the flame had raged within the church, all his other parts had lien open to the fire. And as this man did stick fast in the window, so did the rest stick as fast in the doors that sooner they might have been burned than they could once stir or move one foot; through the which press, at last, there was a way found, that some, going over their heads, got out.

Here also happened another pageant in a certain monk of Gloucester College, whereat Calphurnius might well laugh with open mouth. So it happened that there was a young lad in this tumult, who, seeing the doors fast stopped with the press or multitude, and that he had not way to get out, climbed up upon the door, and there staying upon the top of the door, was forced to tarry still; for to come down into the church again he durst not for fear of the fire, and to leap down toward the street he could not without danger of falling. When he had tarried there awhile, he advised himself what to do; neither did occasion want to serve his purpose; for by chance amongst them that got out over men's heads, he saw a monk coming towards him, who had a great wide cowl hanging at his back. This the boy thought to be a good occasion for him to escape by. When the monk came near unto him, the boy which was in the top of the door came down, and prettily conveyed himself into the monk's cowl, thinking, as it came to pass indeed, that if the monk did escape, he should also get out with him. To be brief, at the last the monk got out over men's heads with the boy in his cowl, and for a great while felt no weight or burden, through the press.

At last, when he was somewhat more come to himself and did shake his shoulders, feeling his cowl heavier than it was accustomed to be, and also hearing the voice of one speaking behind in his cowl, he was more afraid than he was before when he was in the throng, thinking, in very deed, that the evil spirit which had set the church on fire

had flien into his cowl. By and by he began to play
the exorcist: "In the name of God," said he, "and all
saints, I command thee to declare what thou art, that art
behind at my back." To whom the boy answered, "I am
Bertram's boy," for that was his name. "But I," said the
monk, "adjure thee, in the name of the unseparable
Trinity, that thou, wicked spirit! do tell me who thou art,
from whence thou comest, and that thou get thee hence?"
"I am Bertram's boy," said he; "good master, let me go,"
and with that his cowl began to crack upon his shoulders,
with the weight. The monk, when he perceived the
matter, took the boy out, who took to his legs, and ran
away as fast as he could.

Among others, one ran with the church door-key,
beating upon the stone wallo, thinking therewith to break
a hole through to escape.

In the meantime those that were in the streets looking
diligently about them, and perceiving all things to be
safe, marvelled at this sudden outrage, and made signs
and tokens to them that were in the church to keep
themselves quiet, crying to them that there was no
danger.

But, forasmuch as no word could be heard by reason of
the noise that was within the church, those signs made
them much more afraid than they were before, inter-
preting the matter as though all had been on fire without
the church; and for the dropping of the lead and falling
of other things, they should rather tarry still within the
church, and not to venture out. This trouble continued
in this manner by the space of certain hours.

The next day, and also all the following week, there
was an incredible number of bills set up on the church
doors to inquire for things that were lost. "If any man
have found a pair of shoes yesterday in St. Mary's Church,
or knoweth any man that hath found them," etc. Another
bill was set up for a gown that was lost. Another
entreated to have his cap restored. One lost his purse
and girdle, with certain money; another his sword, with
his glove of mail. One inquireth for a ring, and, to be

short, there were few in this garboil but that either through negligence lost, or through oblivion left something behind them.

How few that walk down what has been called the noblest street in Europe, High Street, Oxford; and pass the University Church, lately acquiring fresh notoriety through Newman's Sermons, preached there in the days of Tract 90,—ever imagine that such a highly ridiculous "pageant" was enacted there. But it was, and its date was 1541, and the mighty offence was actually daring to read the Word of God, and understand it in a reasonable way.

CHAPTER XXVI

THE BIBLE-SHUTTERS' CRUELTY

" Man's inhumanity to man
Makes countless thousands mourn."

BURNS.

" His learning turned to casuistry, his accomplishment became cunning,
his bravery fell away into an implacable cruelty. He who had been
open with all men grew into a monster of suspicion. While his eyes
sunk deeper into his head and overlooked nothing, his tongue refused to
speak what his eyes saw. ' If I thought that my cap knew my counsel,
I would throw it in the fire,' he said to Cavendish."

Charles Whibley, speaking of Henry VIII. in his recent edition of
Hall's *Chronicle*. Two beautiful volumes, 1904.

THE story connected with this famous picture from *The
Book and its Story*, by L. N R., is one of the saddest in
literature, and we had better give it here, as a foil to
Foxe's " merry narrative."

The Bibles being set up in St. Paul's by commandment
of the king, and appointment of Bonner, the bishop,
many came to hear them read, not imagining any danger.
Amongst them was John Porter, " a fresh young man and
of a big stature," whose voice could be well heard, so that
he often read aloud, at the wish of the people. All went
well till Cromwell's fall, but soon after that Porter was
sent for, and rebuked sharply.

He answered that he trusted he had done nothing
contrary to the law, but Bonner then said that he had
made expositions upon the text, and there had been
tumults. Porter replied that he trusted that should
not be proved against him. However, Bonner sent him
to Newgate, where he was fettered in irons, both legs
and arms, with a collar of iron about his neck, fastened

to the wall in the dungeon. A relative who came to see him entreated Jewet, then Keeper of Newgate, to release him, and let him go up among the other prisoners, using the money-talisman. But when he came amongst the prisoners, there for felony and murder, he exhorted them to leave their wickedness and blasphemy, and for this was taken down again into the lowest dungeon of all. Here he was oppressed with bolts and irons, and in about a week was found dead.

The night before he died, those that were near that part of the prison, heard him "piteously groaning," and it is supposed that he was again put into "the devil on the neck," which strains and wrenches the neck with the legs together, so that "the more he stirreth in it, the straiter it presseth him."

Well might Bonner have to be hid from the people's fury in Queen Elizabeth's reign, and linger year after year in the Marshalsea Prison, though it is one of the most consoling thoughts that when she came to the throne, there was no retaliation for all the miseries which these first Protestants had endured.

But though, on the one hand, Henry forbade the circulation of the Word of God, after solemnly sanctioning it, and on the other went to the absurdity of writing two books himself to set forth the doctrine which all his subjects were to believe, in which he grossly contradicted himself over and over again, nevertheless he could not undo what had been done, and what he had helped to do. The waves that had broken on the shore were only the precursors of a multitude. He had helped to awaken a mightier sentiment than his own, and in obedience to it the Liturgy was permitted in English two years before his death, and this, says Fuller, was the "farthest pace the Reformation stepped in his reign." *

As for his two books, one was the *Institution of a Christian Man*, which was accepted by Convocation as

* No doubt this was in accordance with Henry's earlier feelings, for, when going to war with France, he had ordered some prayers to be written in English, so that all might understand them.

PORTER READING THE BIBLE IN THE CRYPT OF ST. PAUL'S.
FROM "THE BOOK AND ITS STORY."—L. N. R.

the standard of orthodoxy, and which, with a general leaning towards the Reformers, allowed Seven Sacraments and other Romish doctrines.   This was printed in 1537, and some years afterwards he produced *The Erudition of a Christian Man*, which he published on his own authority without troubling Convocation, and which says that the bread and wine are changed and turned to the very substance of the body and blood.   Whilst the books differ on many points, there is a perfect agreement on one—the passive obedience due to the king in all things, speculative and practical.   Yes, this was his chief religion, and a fine harvest there was by and by for his successor a century later.   His last speech in Parliament was affecting and even eloquent.   It was in December 1545, and after he had spoken of the business of the Session, he paused, hesitated, and finally burst into tears. One thing, he then said, there was specially, in which he could not work alone, and he must call upon them all to help him, in the name and for the honour of Almighty God.   " I hear that the special foundation of our religion, being charity between man and man, is refrigerate, as there was never more dissension and lack of love, the occasions whereof are opinions only and names devised for the continuance of the same.   Some are called Papists, some Lutherans, and some Anabaptists, names devised of the devil, and yet not fully without ground for the severing of one man's heart by conceit of opinion from another.   For the remedy whereof I desire, first, every man of himself to travail for his own amendment. Finally, I exhort nobles and laity not to receive the grace of God in vain, and albeit the Scriptures have been permitted to them in the English tongue, yet not to take upon them the judgment and expositing of the same, but reverently and humbly to receive and use the knowledge which it hath pleased God to show unto them, and in any doubt to resort unto the learned or at best the higher powers.   I am very sorry to know and hear how undeservedly that precious jewel, the Word of God, is disputed, rhymed, sung, and jangled in every alehouse,

house, and tavern. Therefore, as I said before, be in charity one with another, like brother and brother. Then may I justly rejoice that thus long I have lived to see this day; and you, by verity, conscience, and charity between yourselves may in this point, as you have been in divers others, accounted among the rest of the world as blessed men."

There were two parts in this discourse, but as Foxe says, there was one wanting. If he had gone on to suggest the removal of the Act of the Six Articles, then he would have spoken " like a worthy Prince." It was this " Bloody Act " that was the great stumbling-block to Christian charity, and he was largely the author of it. It had set brother against brother, neighbour against neighbour, the superior against the subject, and the wolves to devour the flock of Christ. " And wherein consisteth all this variance, but only because God's Word hath not its free course, but that those who set it forth are condemned and burned ? "

In fact, this speech of the king, in which he exhorted them to set forth God's Word, " both by true preaching and good example giving," should never be read without Foxe's notes on it, and the remembrance that soon afterwards the lovely Anne Askew suffered as few ladies have ever been called to suffer. Foxe sees in such an incident a suitable occasion for summing up the whole controversy of these weary years, and says :

" Princes who exhort to charity and concord do well : but Princes who seek out the causes of discord, and reform the same, do much better. The root and ground of all this grievance riseth hence ; from the prelates and clergy of Rome seeking, as it seemeth, altogether after riches, pomp, and honour of this world ; who, to maintain the same under pretence of religion, do in very deed subvert religion. Under that title of the Church, they bring into the Church manifest errors and absurdities intolerable, who, pretending to be fathers of the Church, if they transgressed but in manners and lightness of life, or negligence of government, they might be borne withal, for peace and concord's sake; and here modesty, civility, quietness, unity, and charity might have place amongst modest natures. But now, they obscure the glory of the Son of God, which in no case ought to be suffered; they extinguish the light and grace of the Gospel; they clog men's conscience; they set up idolatry, and maintain idols; they bring in false invocation, and restrain lawful matrimony, whereby groweth filthy pollution, adultery, and whoredom in the Church unspeakable; they corrupt the Sacraments; they wrest the Scripture to worldly purposes; they kill and persecute God's people; briefly, their doctrine is damnable, their laws be impious, their doings are detestable. And yet, after all this, they creep craftily into the hearts of Princes, under the title of the Church, and colour of concord; making Kings and Princes believe that all be heretics and schismatics who will not be subject to their ordinary power. Now Almighty God, who is a jealous God, and not suffering the glory of His Son to be defaced, nor His truth to be trodden underfoot, stirreth up again the hearts of His people to understand His truth, and to defend His cause. Whereupon of these two parts, as two mighty flints thus smiting together, cometh out the sparkle of this division, which can in no wise be quenched, but that one part must needs yield and give over. There is no neutrality, nor mediation of peace, nor exhortation to agreement, that will serve between these two contrary doctrines, but either the Pope's errors must give place to God's Word, or else the verity of God must give place unto them."

At the close of Henry's reign there was published a *Supplication of the Poor Commons,* somewhat answering to the *Supplication of the Beggars* of twenty years earlier, and to which we have referred. It showed plainly enough what a dreadful state the persecution and bigotry of the time had reduced the realm to, together with the incessant demands for money. It prays the king to study to leave the young prince who would reign after him a Commonwealth to govern, and not an island of brute beasts, among whom the stronger devour the weaker. "They have procured a law that none shall be so hardy as to have the Scripture in his house unless he may spend ten pounds a year. Hath God put immortal souls in none other? Did not Christ send word to John the Baptist that the poor received the Gospel? Why do these men disable them from reading the Scriptures that are not endued with the possessions of the world? Undoubtedly, most gracious Sovereign, because they are the very same that shut the Kingdom of Heaven before men. They enter not in themselves, nor suffer they them to enter that would." Both supplications were published in one book. This reign was not finished, however, before even "Lords a many, and Dukes a few," and all sorts and conditions of men were prohibited from having, taking, or keeping any books "set forth in the names of Fryth, Tyndale, Wickliffe, Joye, Roye, Becon, Bale, Barnes, Coverdale, Turner, or Tracy."

Henry and Luther passed away almost together, Luther one year and Henry the next, the real Defender of the Faith, and the one who was called so by the Pope. Then came five or six years of halcyon quiet under the young and godly Prince Edward, during which the Protestant religion took such firm hold of the mind of the country that Mary and Philip, with all their bloody persecutions, could not greatly disturb it.

It is certainly a relief to part with his Serene Majesty, Henry VIII., and perhaps Fuller is right in saying that all the virtues and vices of all his predecessors from the Conquest were fully represented in him—learning, wisdom, valour, and magnificence; cruelty, avarice, fury, and lust.

And Dantiscus, the Bishop of Vermein, was not far wrong when he wrote to Cranmer that England was passing through such times, in this reign, as had never before happened in any country of the Christian world.

Perhaps there has seldom been such a severe judgment as Lodge's passed upon any ruler, and we cannot subscribe to it:

" We seek in vain for a single act in Henry's life which

might authorise us even to suspect that he had a conscience."

When he was made Defender of the Faith by the Pope, he said he would not lose it for all London, and twenty miles round about it. "Neither is it marvel," exclaimed Tyndale, "for it had cost more than London and forty miles round it is able to make at this hour, beside the effusion of innocent blood."

Yes, the effusion was dreadful in this long reign, and no wonder that Henry was once so haunted by the ghost of one he had unjustly put to death that he left the Army and went home. What home he finally reached we will not venture to say, but it is well for us all to recall at the end of this memorable history what Wolsey once said to him, showing that he was no sycophant. When he was compelled to give up York Place, to the injury of his see, he answered Judge Shelley, who made the demand:

"I charge your conscience, and discharge mine. Howbeit, I pray you, show his Majesty from me, that I most humbly desire his Highness to call to his most gracious rememberance that there is both Heaven and Hell."

EPILOGUE

THE cordial reception given to *Our own English Bible* has encouraged the author thus to proceed, and he hopes to publish a concluding volume on *The Puritan Bible*. Great assistance has been rendered by the Right Honourable Lord Peckover, who not only placed his invaluable collection of Bibles at the author's service, but assisted him with carefully made extracts which are duly acknowledged in the body of the work.

Much valuable help has also been given by the Rev. J. H. Broadbent, B.A. (Lond.), and Mr. W. H. Smalley, which is here thankfully acknowledged.

To the Earl of Leicester the author also presents his thanks for his kind permission to use the unique Coverdale Bible at Holkham Hall.

As to authorities, it would be interminable to quote them, after thirty-five years of reading in the British Museum and other Libraries, but the author has been glad to include some valuable notes from the *Cambridge History of Literature*, just published in time.

Printed by MORRISON & GIBB LIMITED, *Edinburgh*

INDEX

OUR OWN ENGLISH BIBLE

ITS TRANSLATORS AND THEIR WORK.

BY

Rev. W. J. HEATON, B.D., F.R.Hist.S.

With 56 Facsimiles and Illustrations hitherto only found in expensive works.

Crown 8vo, Cloth, Gilt Top.   Price **5s.** *net.*

The History of the first 1500 years,   .   .   .
and the only illustrated work on the subject.

LONDON: F. GRIFFITHS, 34 MAIDEN LANE, STRAND, W.C.

"This is a noble work, and one hitherto greatly needed.   We cordially recommend it to all Bible Lovers who wish to know how we got our Bible.   It is well illustrated with good photographs and drawings."—*British Weekly.*

"Mr. Heaton's volume is a gold mine of information and ought to be widely read. What he says is true, that no Vernacular Bible possesses such a remarkable early history. The illustrations scattered through the text are well chosen."—*Saint Andrew.*

"This story is one which must be dear to every devout heart.   No pains have been spared in the gathering of materials from many quarters, and by lucid description, ample quotation, and excellent pictorial illustrations, there is brought home to the reader a most vivid picture of the long and painful, yet marvellous process by which, on the human side, there has come into our hands that wonderful English Bible which the author fitly describes as the greatest concrete force on the side of truth and righteousness which the world contains."—*Christian.*

"There is a ready market for books about the English Bible.   But the Rev. W. J. Heaton has almost no competition, whilst he has all the popular interest, when he publishes a book on the age before printing.   He tells the difficult story easily, and it is made memorable by many excellent engravings."—*Expository Times.*

"We have been charmed with it from beginning to end.   Where we looked for dry lists, we have found a story more pleasant to read, and more full of interest than many a novel.   It is written for the people, it is true, but its every page bears signs of erudition, research, and skill in handling the facts of history.   Here is at last the romance of the English Bible, for which we have long been waiting."—*Erith Times.*

"The deeply interesting story of a little known period is well told.   Every lover of the English Bible will thank Mr. Heaton as well for the painstaking research which has resulted in the collection of facts of the highest interest as for the skill with which he has marshalled them.   It deserves a wide circulation, and the attractiveness of the volume is greatly increased by a large number of excellent engravings."—*Methodist Recorder.*

THE PURITAN BIBLE

AND OTHER CONTEMPORANEOUS PROTESTANT VERSIONS.

Being the Third Volume of
"OUR OWN ENGLISH BIBLE: ITS TRANSLATORS
AND THEIR WORK."

BY THE

Rev. W. J. HEATON, B.D.

Illustrated with Facsimiles, Portraits, etc.

Crown 8vo, Gilt Top, **6s. 6d.** *net; by post,* **6s. 10d.**

This Volume contains, for the first time, a fairly complete account of those who gave us the Authorised Version. There are also accurate particulars of the Versions used by Queen Elizabeth and Shakespeare.

CONTENTS:—Chapter I. The Boy King.—Chapter II. Sir John Cheke.—Chapter III. Close of the Too Short Reign.—Chapter IV. Queen Mary.—Chapter V. Queen Mary.—Chapter VI. What Befel the Persecuting Wretches.—Chapter VII. The Genevan Bible.—Chapter VIII. Sampson and Gilby.—Chapter IX. Bodley and the Other Helpers.—Chapter X. Its Characteristics.—Chapter XI. A Puritan Production.—Chapter XII. Laurence Tomson.—Chapter XIII. The Bishops' Bible.—Chapter XIV. Alley, Davies, and Becon.—Chapter XV. Bishops' Bible, Perne and Parkhurst.—Chapter XVI. Grindal.—Chapter XVII. Archbishop Sandys.—Chapter XVIII. Horne and Cox.—Chapter XIX. Gabriel Goodman and Others.—Chapter XX. Its Characteristics.—Chapter XXI. Parker's Other Fruitful Labours.—Chapter XXII. The Ultra Puritans and Romanists.—Chapter XXIII. The Authorised Version.—Chapter XXIV. The First Company.—Chapter XXV. The Second Company.—Chapter XXVI. The Third Company.—Chapter XXVII. The Fourth Company.—Chapter XXVIII. The Fifth Company and that for the Apocrypha.—Chapter XXIX. Its Characteristics.—Chapter XXX. English Biblical Versifications.

Over One Hundred Illustrations.

LONDON: FRANCIS GRIFFITHS, 34 MAIDEN LANE, STRAND, W.C.